Remembering
YOUR STORY

Remembering
YOUR STORY

Creating Your Own
Spiritual Autobiography

Revised Edition
Richard L. Morgan

UPPER ROOM BOOKS®
NASHVILLE

REMEMBERING YOUR STORY
Creating Your Own Spiritual Autobiography
Copyright © 2002 by Richard L. Morgan
All rights reserved.

The Upper Room® Web site http://www.upperroom.org
UPPER ROOM®, UPPER ROOM BOOKS® and design logos are trademarks owned by The Upper Room®, Nashville, Tennessee. All rights reserved.

Scripture quotations not otherwise identified are from the New Revised Standard Version of the Bible, copyright 1989, Division of Christian Education of the National Council of the Churches of Christ in the United States of America. Used by permission. All rights reserved.

Scripture quotations designated NIV are taken from the HOLY BIBLE, NEW INTERNATIONAL VERSION. NIV. Copyright 1973, 1978, 1984 by International Bible Society. Used by permission of Zondervan Publishing House. All rights reserved.

Scripture quotations marked CEV are taken from the Contemporary English Version. © 1995 American Bible Society. Used by permission.

Page 174 serves as an extension of this copyright page.

Cover and Interior Design: Ellisor Design

Library of Congress Cataloging-in-Publication Data
Morgan, Richard Lyon, 1929–
    Remembering your story. creating your own spiritual autobiography / Richard L. Morgan.—Rev. ed.
        p. cm.
    Includes bibliographical references and index.
    ISBN 978-0-8358-0963-4
    1. Middle aged persons—Religious life. 2. Autobiography—Religious aspects—Christianity. 3. Storytelling—Religious aspects—Christianity. 4. Christian aged—Religious life. 5. Autobiography—Authorship. 6. Report writing. I. Title. Title.

BV4579.5 .M6652 2002
248.8'4—dc21   2001045440

Printed in the United States of America

**To all story makers and storytellers
and to those who listen**

Special thanks to
sine qua non
editors of Upper Room Books

Rita Collett, JoAnn Miller, Sarah Schaller-Linn, and Denise Duke

without whose persistent and patient editing and listening
the second story of this book would never have come to print.

CONTENTS

FOREWORD

FOR SOME YEARS RICHARD MORGAN has been a part of my story. Our paths have crisscrossed many times, usually at conferences where we find ourselves engaged with others in celebration of the gifts of later life. For both of us, story is central to our understanding of the meaning of life and to our personal and professional journeys. Elsewhere I have written my "credo" or faith statement, which includes the following:

> I believe that the greatest gift we can offer to each other is the telling of and listening to our stories. This empowers us to appropriate and live out our own stories, unifies us in diversity, and leads to reconciliation (the mission of the church).

Jean Shinoda Bolen closes her wonderful midlife spiritual autobiography *Crossing to Avalon* with the following:

> *To bring about a paradigm shift in the culture that will change assumptions and attitudes, a critical number of us have to tell the stories of our personal revelations and transformations....*The stories people tell have a way of taking care of them. If stories come to you, care for them. And learn to give them away where they are needed. Sometimes a person needs a story more than food to stay alive.[1]

A GUIDE FOR RECOLLECTING THE STORY

While some folks find it easy to get in touch with their stories, it is not easy for all of us. Dick mentions in his preface that he and I have talked about the need for a resource designed for those who are convinced about the importance of doing this work but do not know where to begin or how to proceed. Here is such a guidebook with enough variety to be useful to many persons in diverse situations.

Dick has chosen to offer this guidebook for persons working in a group context. This seems wise; having companions on this journey helps when we run into rough spots on the road, get stuck in the ditch, or lose heart. The journey, while infinitely valuable, is not easy. Going with others makes the journey possible for some who might not stay the course without support.

Furthermore, something holy happens when we gather in groups for this sacred work. A group is more than the sum of its members; we discover when we gather that God is in our very midst. When we share from what feels like our deepest, most intimate and personal place, we paradoxically connect to what is most universally bonding.

I once attended an open meeting of Alcoholics Anonymous. A man sitting near me listened intently as a speaker gave a moving description of the power of group support. Then he leaned over to me and said, "She's telling my story." At the deepest level, with this kind of story sharing, we discover that we are telling and listening to both our own and one another's stories simultaneously.

Parts of our story are unfinished, painful, in need of healing. Dick provides many opportunities to bring healing to the wounds, completion to the unfinished parts, forgiveness to self and others. One of the most powerful chapters is the one on healing of memories.

This book is eclectic in the best sense of the term—made up of the best things, selected from diverse sources. Dick has brought together useful models from evangelism programs; family therapy; crisis intervention; death and dying; gerontology; professional caregiving; spiritual direction; theology; and the worlds of poetry, fiction, and mythology.

The separate leader's guide is a useful feature of this study. It gives tools the leader can use to provide structure for the group, from suggested time frames for each exercise to supplementary materials.

OTHER USES

While this book's primary purpose is for use with groups, an individual who feels a call to do this work either alone or with a spiritual director, mentor, or other support person would find this a helpful resource. The exercises are easily adapted to work in solitude, as are the prayers. Thus even for persons who prefer to do their story-recollecting alone or who do not have access to a group, this book offers significant help.

This resource book contains an outline for the videotaping of someone's reminiscences. One could employ this adaptation of the model in a nursing home, as an intergenerational activity in a congregation, as a way of saving part of one's family story, and in many other ways.

Dick's focus is the capturing of story, both for one's personal growth and for sharing with close friends and family. Use the book as a tool for training persons of any age for intentional evangelism. Mastering the techniques of discovering one's story and its connection with the story of the people of God is a necessary prerequisite to sharing one's story with those outside the community of faith.

Since its publication in 1996, this book has been used across the nation in different situations and with diverse audiences. The revision reflects some of the experiences of those whose lives have been changed by creating their own spiritual autobiography. I found the revised Leader's Guide a creative way to use this book in many situations, whether for older persons or people of different generations.

CLOSING THOUGHTS

The network of those interested in aging and the spiritual journey, those interested in discovering the connections between their story and *the* Story will find in this book a rich resource. Dick Morgan has been generous in the sharing of his own journey and its meanings, both at conferences and in his writings. Here he gives us a marvelous array of tools for doing this work on our own journeys and with others. May God's blessing be with him and with each of us who use this book, now and always.

—LYNN W. HUBER
ACSW, Ph.D.
Coordinator: The Stillpoint School for Spiritual Formation
and Spiritual Direction

PREFACE

SINCE THE TIME OF *REMEMBERING YOUR STORY'S* first publication, the practice of remembering and recording stories has become a national movement. Michael Vitez, writing for the *Philadelphia Inquirer*, comments,

> Across the country, older Americans—from the robust to the dying—are writing down their stories or telling them for others to record. Some end up as published books....Others go no further than handwritten pages in a spiral notebook.
>
> Whatever the form, the purpose is usually the same: *to pass along a legacy to one's children and grandchildren—and to find meaning in one's life* (italics mine).[1]

It all began for me in listening to life stories in the nursing home. I remember visiting in a nursing home; a dear lady stopped me and said, "People seldom listen to my stories, so I've stopped trying to tell them." I recorded her life story, and her story sparked the first *Remembering Your Story* group in a nursing home.

From that humble beginning, the concern for telling and preserving one's life story has spread like a ripple effect, first to churches, where members of different ages gathered to discover community through story sharing. These groups met at different times and places and for different reasons, but the common thread was community through story sharing.

Only recently has sharing stories become a major concern for those who work in hospice settings, both for staff and volunteers, and as a way to help dying persons be in touch with the meaning of their lives. Another development focused on intergenerational activities in the parish. It was discovered that stories connect generations. The wisdom and experience of older persons were shared with younger generations, and older persons listened to the stories and issues of younger generations.

Why this growing interest in sharing life stories? For older persons medical technology has prolonged life and given more time for review of their story. American life and culture are changing so fast that older people realize that their grandchildren have no idea of the events that shaped their lives. And more and more midlifers are realizing that with the increased mobility of modern life, family stories that once were passed down orally will be lost if not preserved.

My hope and prayer are that those who enter the world of spiritual auto-biography will discover the incredible power of sharing spiritual stories. As we find ourselves drawn by God into telling our stories, we become creative agents of meaning. Then like Jacob, who wrestled with his story (and God) at a place called Bethel, we can awaken from sleep and cry, "Surely the Lord is in this place [my life]—and I did not know it!" (Gen. 28:16).

I am reminded of the first lines of a poem that Elizabeth Barrett Browning wrote on October 17, 1856, at the age of fifty—just five years before her death.

> *Of writing many books there is no end;*
> *And I, who have written much in prose and verse*
> *For others' uses, will write now for mine,—*
> *Will write my story for my better self,*
> *As when you paint your portrait for a friend,*
> *Who keeps it in a drawer, and looks at it*
> *Long after he [or she] has ceased to love you, just*
> *To hold together what he [or she] was and is.*

Join me in remembering your story, and leave a self-portrait, holding together who you were and are. Then you will be able to answer life's great questions: Did my life really matter? Was my time well spent? and Where did God meet me in life's journey?

Let this be our prayer as we begin this sacred journey:

> *O God,*
> *The beginning of any task leads us to you, as does its ending.*
> *You are beginning and end.*
> *We ask for your grace as we begin this incredible journey.*
> *We ask you to stay with us*
> *as we journey through our life stories and listen to others,*
> *confident that "the one who began a good work among [us]*
> *will bring it to completion by the day of Jesus Christ."*
> *Amen.*

FROM MEMORY TO FAITH: LIFE STORIES

"Remember the days of old,
consider the years long past;
ask your father, and he will inform you;
your elders, and they will tell you."
—DEUTERONOMY 32:7

God hold you in this turning,
Christ warm you through this night,
Spirit breathe its ancient rhythm,
Peace give your sorrows flight.
—JAN L. RICHARDSON

We sat and talked, and he told me some of his story. He was only a heartbeat from retirement, and he approached that moment with constant dread. "I've been in charge of a large company for years," he said. "But soon I'll be a nobody. Those golden handshakes will become golden handcuffs." Successful, affluent, and in excellent health, this man still had a quarter of his life to live. But he faced those autumn years with a nagging sense of not being needed; he had no goals for all that free time, and he was experiencing a pervasive sense of impending doom. He raised two haunting questions: "What will I do with these last years of my life?" and "What has my life really meant?"

Somehow those questions reflect the way many persons feel as they reach retirement and face the challenge of longer life. Medical science has given us the means to prolong life without providing the meaning for these years. These concerns become part of the texture of all our life stories, no matter what the age.

Retirement years can provide precious time to cultivate the inner life, but we persist in cramming our days full of endless activities in an attempt to wallpaper over the empty spaces within. These years hold the promise of being our best years, years when we live life to the fullest. Yet often they end in depression, meaninglessness, and a gnawing sense that we are simply waiting for death.

One way out of this spiritual wasteland is to discover the meaning of our life by remembering our story, connecting with God's story, and listening to another's story. When we remember our stories together, the acts of listening and telling help us move beyond the normal boundaries we impose on ourselves. We gain deeper insight into the ways of God's grace in other people and in ourselves.

Any age is a good age to reflect on the story of your life. Midlife, where a rich store of experience is available, is a significant time to review, pause, and prepare for a long future with assurance and optimism.

My twelve-year-old son Christopher was captivated by stories of the sinking of the *Titanic*. He read books about the disaster and even made a model of the *Titanic* for a science project in school. But his eyes gleamed when I told him that his great-great grandfather, G. Campbell Morgan, was a personal friend of Captain Smith. And when I gave him the handwritten sermon notes that his great-great grandfather preached on the sinking of the *Titanic*, he responded, "Awesome!" So the sermon notes on the sinking of *Titanic* had spanned four generations and would be preserved for generations yet to come.

When my siblings and I were children, we sat around the dinner table with parents and grandparents and told our stories. At meal's end, the dessert plates were pushed aside, and we asked, "Do you remember when...?" and lively conversation ensued as family members shared the stories. Often a grandparent would share stories of a world we never knew: of pioneer days, the Great Depression, and World Wars. Grandparents were the story keepers, the ones who handed on the family values and traditions.

Now the artificial images families watch on television have little to do with family stories or values. The stories and values are lost in the maelstrom of our busy lives and distracted lifestyles. So remembering our stories is not just for our own benefit; it is a sacred responsibility to hand on our values and faith to coming generations.

As you begin the task of remembering your story, consider the seven basic principles that are essential for this journey of faith.

> ## FOUNDATION PRINCIPLES OF SPIRITUAL AUTOBIOGRAPHY
>
> **1.** Every life is a unique, invaluable story.
>
> **2.** God speaks to us in our stories.
>
> **3.** Connecting our stories with God's Story is the work of the Spirit.
>
> **4.** Painful memories can be healed through stories.
>
> **5.** Remembering our stories creates community and the future.
>
> **6.** Faith stories are the legacy we leave.
>
> **7.** Stories create meaning... at any age.
>
>

1. EVERY LIFE IS A UNIQUE, INVALUABLE STORY

Many persons believe that their stories are uninteresting or unimportant. They claim that only celebrities have colorful, meaningful stories to tell. They say, "I'm not important enough. Who would be interested in my story?" Yet every life is worthy of a novel. Why? Because it is a unique, once-told tale. It is your story or my story, and no one else has ever lived it. As Henri Nouwen has expressed it in *The Life of the Beloved*, "Your life and my life are, each of them, one-of-a-kind. No one has ever lived your life or my life before, and no one will live them again. Our lives are unique stones in the mosaic of human existence—priceless and irreplaceable."[1]

One only needs to read the Gospel narratives to see how Jesus valued every person's story, ordinary stories that sound so contemporary: a widow grieving the loss of her only son; a disturbed man, abandoned by the community, living alone; a woman at a well, her life like shards of a broken jug; a man sick for thirty-eight years, who began to enjoy his sickness and the care of others; a man with honest doubt who needed reassurance.

2. GOD SPEAKS TO US IN OUR STORIES

It is in our stories that God speaks to us. As Frederick Buechner has said in *Telling Secrets*, "Maybe nothing is more important than that we keep track, you and I, of these stories of who we are and where we have come from and the people we have met along the way because it is precisely through these stories in all their particularity...that God makes [God's] self known to each of us most powerfully and personally."[2]

Remembering our stories is more than reminiscence or recalling our past. Listening to our life is like listening to the voice of God, even as the boy Samuel thought Eli was calling him, only to realize that God was speaking to him.

Stories have power. The Kalahari Desert bushmen believe that their stories contain their soul as a people. They tell their stories only to those they trust; if an enemy comes into possession of their stories, the enemy will have the power to destroy them spiritually.

I interpret this Kalahari understanding of story as referring to the individual as well as the whole community. Stories present powerful means of communicating at all levels. Though many storytellers use the same words, gestures, and inflections each time they tell the story, each telling is unique because of the audience and the circumstances.

Remembering our stories helps us perceive ways God has shared in our personal history. We remember incredible answers to prayer and grace moments, times when God helped us through what seemed impossible crises.

3. CONNECTING OUR STORIES WITH GOD'S STORY IS THE WORK OF THE SPIRIT

Another dimension of remembering our stories is the connecting of our stories with God's story in scripture. Scripture records experiences of God's presence. We must keep in mind that the stories of the biblical tradition and our personal stories are not all that different. The Bible is a collection of stories about ordinary people in ordinary places doing ordinary things, when the Extraordinary happens to them. When we take our stories seriously enough to explore and share them, they can become places of divine revelation. If spirituality means "living in the Spirit," then remembering our stories leads to spiritual formation.

In telling and listening to the Gospel stories, Christians can more readily identify times of God's presence in their own lives. In his book *Story Journey*, Thomas Boomershine states that "if the adventures of the Gospel are learned deeply, our stories are woven together with Jesus' story."[3]

We hear the biblical story and say, "That's my story too"; and as we remember our stories, we recall God's story. Some memory of God's presence in our lives reminds us of a story from scripture. As we connect our stories with the biblical witness, we become aware of new revelations and of times when God's extraordinary love became known in something very ordinary. God's spirit makes the connection. As Jesus promised those first disciples and us, "But the Counselor, the Holy Spirit, whom the Father will send in my name, will teach you all things and will remind you of everything I have said to you" (John 14:26, NIV).

In the busyness of early adult years, our emphasis on achieving and spending can strip life of its spiritual quality. We may discern the work of the Spirit in our stories only in later age as we look back on the whole sweep of our life with the eyes of faith. Our story merges with God's story whenever we perceive God as the "silent companion" in life's journey.

4. PAINFUL MEMORIES CAN BE HEALED THROUGH STORIES

Some people resist remembering their stories, because memories of painful events in the past seem best left there. The journey down memory lane is not always pleasant. Wrong turns, dead ends, stupid blunders, and careless actions torment us. We may say, "I lived through that once; it really hurt; and I don't want to think about it anymore." Furthermore, we discover family skeletons rattling around in the closets of our lives, and some of us believe those scary memories need to be kept there.

Experience proves that those memories will resurface, because they always remain a part of who we are. But instead of being a burden of guilt and remorse, even the most painful experiences, once we have made peace with them, can become sources of blessing and strength for life's journey. Remembering our stories can help us experience that even if our present story is broken, it can be made whole.

5. REMEMBERING OUR STORIES CREATES COMMUNITY AND THE FUTURE

When God created the world, only one time did God say, "It is not good," and that was, "It is not good that the man should be alone." Although you can preserve your story in solitude through personal journaling, being in a group that shares stories is a powerful way to be in touch with your own story.

These stories fill us with a holy wonder and gratitude for God's presence in every life. Indeed, shared stories become "holy ground." Thomas Hart states in *The Art of Christian Listening*:

> There is nothing quite so sacred, so fragile, or so mysterious as the human being. There is probably no service we can render other persons quite as great or important as to be listener and receiver to them in those moments when they need to open their hearts and tell someone their story.[4]

Listening to others' stories is a gift we offer them. But we also receive a gift as we realize that every story is in some way the story of us all. Despite details and events that make our individual stories unique, there are moments when we recognize our story in the stories of others. Some experience, celebrative event, or difficult moment in another's story resonates with our story, and we begin to recognize our oneness. *People who share their stories become soul friends, bound together in unique ways.* This being bound together may reflect Luke's meaning: "All the believers were together and had everything in common" (Acts 2:44, NIV). Nouwen says,

> [Listening] is like weaving a new pattern with two different lifestories stretched out on the same loom. After a story is told and received with care, the lives of two people have become different. Two people have discovered their own unique stories and two people have become an integral part of a new fellowship.[5]

This weaving also occurs in small groups where the church, the true *koinonia* or fellowship, comes into being as our stories connect with other persons' stories and with God's story.

Remembering your story also gives direction for the rest of your story. Sharing stories is not simply a matter of recalling or clinging to the past. Søren Kierkegaard said, "Life can only be understood backwards; but it must be lived forwards," which reminds me of an exchange between a tourist and an old farmer.

"Have you lived here all your life?" the tourist asked.

"No," replied the farmer. "Not yet!"

We continue to realize that our stories are incomplete and that the next chapter of the story remains a mystery to be experienced. One of the rewards of remembering our story is to find direction for our last years. When Moses counseled the Israelites to "remember the long way that the LORD your God has led you these forty years in the wilderness" (Deut. 8:2), he was not just giving them a gentle reminder. He was urging them to let that same God lead them in their new journey into the land of promise.

6. Faith Stories Are the Legacies We Leave

Imagine that you are visiting your mother's house. While poking around in the attic, you come across a dusty shoebox tucked under the eaves. Curious, you open the box to discover sheets of yellow stationery—letters written by your grandmother. You can almost hear her quavering voice as you read stories about her...and you. Or imagine coming into possession of an old family Bible in which you find *underlined* verses with brief comments by your grandfather in the margin. You suddenly become aware of how God was present in his life.

What if you wrote your life story and hid it in a desk drawer? or saved it on a floppy disk? or videotaped it and hid it away for later discovery? What a treasure for future generations! Your story is your legacy.

We live in a time of age segregation. We see it everywhere. The greatest wedge dividing generations is the American practice of segregating groups by age—toddlers with toddlers, teens with teens, older persons with older persons. Furthermore, in many cases, activities that once pulled families together—caring for frail elders, minding small children, and telling family stories—are either disregarded or relegated to professionals, institutions, or government-funded service providers.

Listening to one another's stories may be the way to connect generations: young people listening to the wisdom of the elders, older people really hearing the stories youth tell about their lives. Stories can help us see beyond age and gender and realize we are all children of God.

7. STORIES CREATE MEANING...AT ANY AGE

At any age, if we are to face life with integrity and purpose, we must know that our lives do mean something, that we matter to someone, and that whatever story we have lived, it has brought us to this point. Carl Jung showed that sense of meaning when he wrote, "Much might have been different if I myself had been different. But it was as it had to be; for all came about because I am as I am."[6]

Recall the Gospel story of the woman in the crowd who had been sick for twelve years. She had become a nonperson, without hope of healing through normal avenues. From the wounded center of her life, she reached out in desperate hope to touch Jesus. "Who touched me?" he asked. Even in a crowd Jesus knew the touch of faith. He said to her, "Daughter, your faith has made you well; go in peace" (Luke 8:48). She had been known as a sick person, but Christ's transforming touch restored her to wholeness and personhood.

Remembering our story helps us journey into wholeness. In the process of remembering and sharing our stories, we restore those parts of ourselves we have forgotten, suppressed, or denied. We discover that we can reconceptualize and that even the difficult memories become moments of God's grace. As we touch the stories of Christ and connect them with our stories, we find wholeness.

Erik Erikson, whose classic work *Childhood and Society* depicted eight stages of humanity, believed that a person's final task—particularly in the later years—is that of achieving integrity; that is, accepting life as it has been lived. Integrity describes a person who has adapted to all of life and who has found a sense of wholeness and peace. This person recognizes life's "dangers, toils, and snares" but affirms that life is worthwhile when seen in the light of God's grace.

Remembering our stories is a way to see beyond the roles we have played to reaffirm our true personhood. Granted, we spend our lives looking at a "cloudy picture in a mirror" (1 Cor. 13:12, CEV) and only see "face-to-face" in the next life. But remembering our stories helps us stay in touch with who we really are, instead of the roles we play or have played. In all of life's experiences we respond to definite role expectations from job, family, friends, and culture. With older age, retirement or debility strips many of these role expectations from us.

As we get in touch with our stories, we gain a sense of who we really are, the person we must be now. In a way, our life stories are like quilting. Our lives resemble a patchwork quilt. We start with scraps of material passed on to us: our genetic makeup, our family history and traditions. Then we add other materials with the talents and opportunities we've been given. Each story we tell is like a piece of quilt block that represents one bit of color or one piece of texture.

Finally we take all these pieces of material and put them together, and they become a unique pattern of our own making. When pieced together the stories become a beautiful quilt. Stories heal us as we remember the diverse fragments and witness the piecing together of the quilt.

Edith Sinclair Downing understood her life as a "coming together" as evidenced in her hymn lyrics "As We Look Back in Memory":

> As we look back in memory on our life's tapestry,
> The past weaves into the present, and precious scenes we see.
> A song brings us remembrance of friends from long ago.
> A letter carries treasures; a child's face brings a glow.
>
> Some memories bring sorrow of hurts that are long past.
> Regret and guilt stay with us; we fear that failures last.
> Yet all we weave has meaning, each thought, each deed, a strand.
> The bright and darker colors reveal God's gracious plan.
>
> O Timeless Wondrous Weaver, You weave Your perfect will.
> The threads of gold that glisten display your matchless skill.
> And when our fingers falter at our life's eventide,
> You turn our weaving over, and show the other side!

There is a sense of urgency about preserving one's faith story in the later years. It is sad when older people wait too long to achieve this task. As the writer of Ecclesiastes stated, "Remember your creator in the days of your youth, before the days of trouble come, and the years draw near when you say, 'I have no pleasure in them'" (Eccles. 12:1). We might well rephrase those words in this way: Remember...your story in the days when you can write it down, before the inevitable losses of old age come, and you can no longer fulfill that task. Matilda Johansen, age 101, expresses this thought in her own words:

> Here I am, an old woman already. I always thought I had a book inside me. Every year I told myself, "Next year you'll write your book." The years came and went. It always seemed like next year I'd start on it, but I never did—and I've had a whole century. If you have a book inside you, sit down and get it written. It's not a matter of having the time. If you want to do something badly enough, you do it. You set other things aside, and you make it a priority. You stop giving your life away to obligations. Now my hands are twisted up with arthritis, and I can't see beyond the end of my nose. See? I have the time, but now I can't do it.[7]

In *Hymns to an Unknown God*, Sam Keen urges each person to "examine the sacred text of your daily experience, reconstruct the events and relationships that went into the creation of your being, re-collect memories and form them into narratives that make your life a once-told tale."[8]

I invite you to take this journey of faith, this journey into wholeness. You may work alone in the silence of your soul, or you may join a group that shares stories. No one knows where this journey will lead you, but one thing is sure: God will join you on this journey. Let the following poem inspire you as you begin this sacred journey.

AN UNTOLD STORY: GROUP PROCESS AS A PILGRIMAGE

RICHARD L. MORGAN

In the midst of struggles, silence, and stress

We gather as pilgrims in a new land

to explore our stories

and the space /that separates us from one another.

The air is tense with anxiety

as the journey into the unknown begins.

We all have stories to tell;

Some we know, others locked within our hearts.

But we are our story.

We wonder,

Will all who sit here understand and accept my story?

Or will the episodes from my past

Not be heard...or understood?

I realize the group in which I move

Has power to create, reveal, and heal

all in a one-time unique way.

I am afraid and yet hopeful,

Alive in the presence of myself and others.

THE SPIRITUAL LIFELINE

"A wandering Aramean was my ancestor; he went down into Egypt and lived there as an alien....When the Egyptians treated us harshly and afflicted us,...we cried to the Lord, the God of our ancestors....The Lord brought us out of Egypt...and gave us this land"

—DEUTERONOMY 26:5-9

Telling the story of our lives is one of the most important activities of the later years. It reminds us that we are still emerging, growing people. It shows us how we have changed and how we have been transformed....[Life review] is...a stabilization in the security of the past so that we can go beyond to embrace the future.

— JANE MARIE THIBAULT

*M*aggie Kuhn, that indomitable founder of the Gray Panthers, urged the church to help older adults do a life review. This life review helps persons realize the ways they have coped and survived major changes in society, as well as helps in a personal way: "By recalling past accomplishments and half-forgotten skills, memories can motivate and give new energy."[1] A spiritual life review not only helps people embrace their past history; it provides a real challenge as to what to include in the rest of life. A *spiritual* life review can broaden one's vision at any age and can serve as a critical tool with which to approach life.

A unique way to do spiritual life review is by creating a spiritual life-line, which serves as a time map for organizing a person's insights about his or her history of spirituality. By design it not only helps persons make contact with their past, but it allows them to get in touch with what they can become, regardless of the time that remains.

Dan Wakefield in *The Story of Your Life* says, "To draw a map of our spiritual journey is to look for the experiences and changes, the turning points, triumphs and crashes, dark nights and mountain peaks we have traversed to become the kind of person we are."[2] Consider making a road map of your life story.

Prepare to draw your road map by securing a large piece of paper and lots of crayons or markers. Think about it at first, perhaps taking a few notes on how you will draw the road map and what you might include. Using a different color for varying life experiences may give visibility to some of your perceptions. Give it whatever shape or form you want; map out what feels natural for you, the way your life seems to unfold. What surfaces as you recall the events of your life may surprise or upset you. Take time to be present to whatever arises as you draw your road map of life. Pray for guidance, patience, tolerance, and love as you prepare to undertake this exercise.

WHAT MIGHT YOUR ROAD MAP LOOK LIKE?

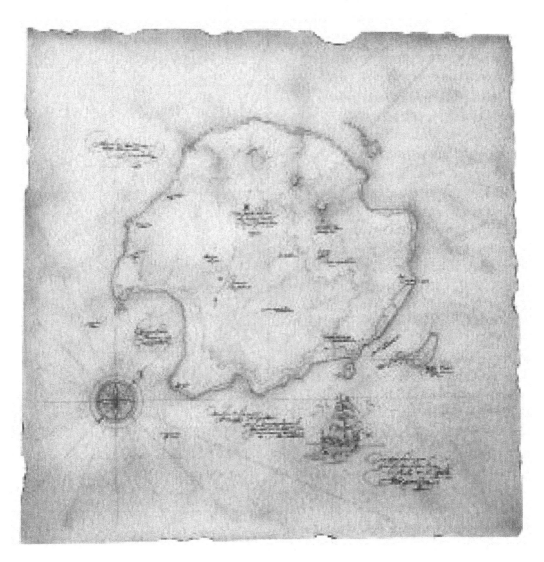

The "Seasons of One's Life" calendar divides our lives into twelve calendar months, each month lasting seven years. (For example, the month of May represents ages 29–35, the month of October ages 64–70.)

Circle your current month. How does that make you feel?

In the space allowed, briefly jot down words or phrases that represent some significant moments in your life story thus far.

Every seven years are like a month in the years of a lifeline. When you look at January, you begin with childhood years. At the end of January, you are seven years old, in second grade, and get your second teeth. You reach teen years in February, and in March you are 21. You can vote; you're in the world. In May, June, and July you're establishing yourself in career and family. At the end of September, you're beginning to think about your later years, how you will spend October, November, and December.

Choose one of the months of your life story (representing a seven-year period of your life), and tell about a significant moment in those years. For example, if you choose March, you might want to tell about your wedding day. Or if it is July, relate a significant career change or a child's graduation from college.

Recall the cycles of your life story in seven-year periods, each representing a month of the year.	
January	0–7 years
February	8–14 years
March	15–21 years
April	22–28 years
May	29–35 years
June	36–42 years
July	43–49 years
August	50–56 years
September	57–63 years
October	64–70 years
November	71–77 years
December	78–X years

SEASONS OF ONE'S LIFE

SIGNIFICANT MOMENT

REMEMBERING YOUR STORY BY THE PLACES YOU HAVE LIVED

Another way to gain a perspective on your life story without focusing on any one experience is to remember the places you have lived in your life.

 LIFE MAP EXERCISE

1. On a piece of 8" x 14" paper, place a large A (alpha) in the middle of the extreme left of the sheet.

2. Below the letter A write your birth year.

3. Across the sheet (on the right side) place a large T (Today) and write today's date (year).

4. List all the homes where you have lived, including towns and dates.

5. Create a memory flow by noting on the bottom of the page memories associated with these places. Include happy and sad memories.

6. Choose the memories that are turning points in your story.

7. Chart the turning points between A and T (birth and today's date), creating a life map. Your life map might look like this:

A
1940

T
2002

Lexington, KY 1940-48	Phila., PA 1949-59	Richmond, VA 1961-71	Raleigh, NC 1972-90	Greensboro, NC 1990--
childhood Kentucky Derby baptism	teen years college	first job marriage children	career change divorce	second marriage career change church change

Turning Points

1949 (age 9) Move to Philadelphia	1961 (age 21) First Job, Family	1982 (age 42) Divorce	1990 (age 50) Move, Second Marriage, New career

The spiritual journey of Moses could be viewed through the decisive turning points of his story: rescue from the Nile River in Egypt, flight to Midian; burning bush experience, exodus from Egypt and crossing of the Red Sea, wilderness experience, and death on Mount Nebo.

THE SPIRITUAL LIFELINE

Now that you have begun looking at your life story, you are ready to do the spiritual lifeline exercise. This exercise is much more involved and becomes the foundation of remembering your story. You may choose to discuss this exercise and your insights with a partner. "Doing" your spiritual lifeline is an ongoing task throughout this study.

The spiritual lifeline provides a panoramic view of your life story. As you think of your life, in your mind's eyes let your view stretch from horizon to horizon. Don't stop and visit any place yet. Let your spirit's eye keep moving as what you remember begins to take the shape of stories.

 1 Draw a horizontal line across a piece of paper. The horizontal line represents your spiritual lifeline.

On your lifeline write the following in black or blue ink:

At the extreme left of the line, write the year of your birth. Write it in large numerals, since this is the year your history began.

At the extreme right of the line, write the year you think you're going to die and your age at that time (predicted death). A simple way to guess that date is to add the number of years you will live to your birth date, so that if you're born in 1940, and you predict you'll live to be 90, your predicted death year is 2030.

Put an X on your lifeline to represent where you are now, that is, the present year.

Your spiritual lifeline might look like this:

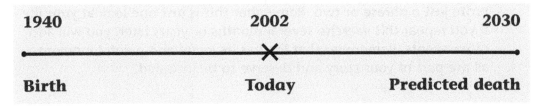

1940	2002	2030
Birth	Today	Predicted death

Take a moment to reflect quietly on your perceptions thus far, especially the realization of the time that remains in your lifeline. Consider the significant historical events you have lived through since your birth. You may or may not remember them in chronological order but plan to list these events chronologically. Reflect on the significance of these events. Make notes or record your thoughts in a journal. You may wish to discuss these events with a friend.

2 Acknowledge that every life story has its ups and downs, its celebrations and crises—in the past, the present, and the future.

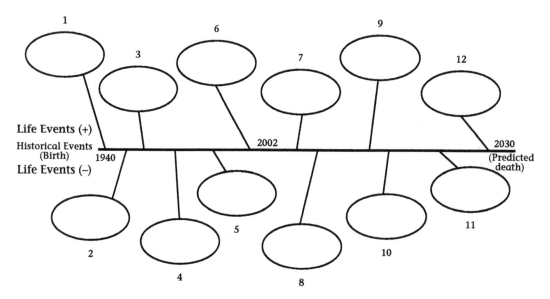

Draw three to five small ovals above and below the line.

Jot down in a phrase or two some of the celebrative moments of your life in the ovals above the lifeline.

Jot down some of your crises in the ovals below the lifeline.

Write just a phrase or two. Remember this is just one look at your life. If you repeat this exercise several months or years later, you will add other events. Remember that life has its joyful and painful moments; all are part of your story and deserve to be included.

TheSpiritualLifeline

3 Think of life as a whole. In his book *A Search for God in Time and Memory*, John S. Dunne states that in "composing a personal creed...the object of the search would be your God...to know what you personally believe in and act upon."[3]

Reflect again on your celebrative and painful life events. Can you now discern where God was present in those moments? Consider if any of those events changed, broadened, or narrowed your concept of God.

Recall the times you needed God the most—times you felt God was with you, times you felt angry at God or abandoned by God, times when you wanted to praise God. In red ink beside the events on the lifeline jot down some of your thoughts or feelings about where God was present in your life story.

John Dunne says that life is a walk from a point on the circumference of a circle to its center. The center of the circle represents our most integrated self. Dunne invites us to imagine a circle so large that each person has a place to stand on the circumference of the circle. As we stand on the circumference, we only partially know ourselves; as we begin the journey toward the center, we come to know ourselves more clearly and deeply.

All of us must take this journey to the center by ourselves, but we find ourselves relating to many others on a similar journey. As we make this pilgrimage of faith, we come closer to God.

4 Focus on "grace moments"—moments when God was present in your life story. Raise the following questions about your grace moments:

- What was the moment?

- Who were the significant people involved?

- What were your feelings?

- What were the consequences?

- Where did God fit into this situation?

PAUL'S SPIRITUAL LIFELINE

The Book of Acts records two accounts of Paul's spiritual lifeline. Paul's defense before the Jews at Jerusalem (Acts 22:1-21) and Paul's speech before King Agrippa (Acts 26:1-23) record Paul's spiritual journey. In his second letter to the Corinthians Paul records more of his spiritual autobiography (read 2 Cor. 11:21-33).

Based on these biblical records, Paul's spiritual lifeline would look like this:

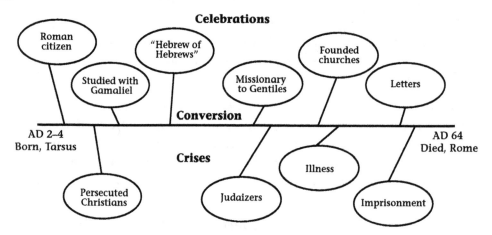

In a real sense, Paul wrote his spiritual lifeline in his letters to the churches, as he reflected on his life story. In his letter to the church at Philippi, written late in his life and while in prison at Rome, he cataloged all the positive aspects of his earlier life (Phil. 3:4-6). At that point he realized that "whatever gains I had, these I have come to regard as loss because of Christ. More than that, I regard everything as loss because of the surpassing value of knowing Christ Jesus my Lord" (Phil. 3:7-8).

Although Paul prayed constantly that his "thorn in the flesh" would be removed (2 Cor. 12:1-9), later he realized that this suffering had brought about his understanding of the truth of God's words, "My grace is sufficient for you, for power is made perfect in weakness" (2 Cor. 12:9).

As you work through your life story in the ensuing chapters, you may return to your spiritual lifeline and expand what you have written. In closing, spend some time in silence and then pray the "Prayer of Thanksgiving for the Seasons of Life" by Sarah Hipps:

Dear Lord, thank you for your presence with us through all the seasons of life...through the times of milk and honey and through our wanderings in the wilderness.

Thank you, Lord, for your potter's hands at work in all of life.

Lord, we give thanks for children; for their boundless energy, their curiosity, their love, their openness, their joy of life.

Thank you, Lord, for your potter's hands at work with children.

Lord, we give thanks for young adults; for their growing search to build meaningful lives, for their new ideas and approaches to the problems of society, for their children and the loving families they seek to build.

Thank you, Lord, for your potter's hands at work with young adults who are beginning their life's work.

Lord, we give thanks for those in the middle of life; for the families they have guided into adulthood, for the life work they have built and sustained, for the faith they have nurtured in others, for the presence they provide as they walk life's path with their parents and older friends.

Thank you, Lord, for your potter's hands at work with those in the middle of life.

Lord, we give thanks for those grown up and grown older; for the experiences they have survived, for the wisdom with which they have been blessed, for the spiritual richness of their lives, for their witness of faith.

Thank you, Lord, for your potter's hands at work with those grown to the fourth age.

Lord, we give thanks for the cloud of witnesses that has gone before us, leaving their imprint of life and faith upon each of us...and upon your world.

Thank you, Lord, for your potter's hands at work with those who have gone before us.

Creator God, we are indeed thankful that in each stage of life you bless us with your presence. At every age...and especially in old age, you mold and shape us with your potter's hands into people with purpose and value who can reach out to others, touching humanity with the love that only you can give us.

Praise be to God. Amen.

THE RIVER OF LIFE

All streams run to the sea, but the sea is not full;
to the place where the streams flow,
there they continue to flow.
—ECCLESIASTES 1:7

There is a river whose streams
make glad the city of God.
—PSALM 46:4

But how can we ever be healed theologically,
individually, unless we refuse to accept a split in
our own selves between what is publicly and what
is privately acceptable—until we can find a way
to tell our own stories, hear one another's stories,
and learn to tell them again in new ways?
—ROBERTA C. BONDI

*O*ur road maps of life and spiritual lifelines have helped us get in touch with the unfolding story of our lives. However, all too often we block out the right side of our brains—the intuitive, mystical, spontaneous, holistic part of ourselves. During our working lives we are more verbal, rational, and goal-oriented people. Doing is more important than being. We are more comfortable with the rational, the provable, the known. However, God has given us the gift of imagination and fantasy to bring us closer to the creative Spirit.

ACTIVATING THE RIGHT BRAIN

Older adulthood sometimes frees persons from conforming to this world's demands for productivity and achievement. Often we fail to realize that, at any age, we can be transformed by "the renewing" of our minds. We can all discover depths of spirituality unknown to us as we activate the right side of our brains and explore the limitless possibilities of our imagination. In his book *Adventure Inward,* Morton Kelsey wrote,

> Spiritual discovery, making a direct and creative encounter with spiritual reality, may well depend on developing one's imaginative capabilities. We have two hemispheres of the brain, one dealing with logic and language and the other with images, shapes, art and story. If we are to be whole people we need to learn to use both sides of the brain and deal with our imaginative capacities. The images arising from the depths of us in dreams or fantasies or intuitions are one way by which we are brought into contact with the spiritual world. Without the use of images and imagination it is nearly impossible to obtain knowledge of the depth of ourselves or of the spiritual reality beyond us.[1]

Americans are a pragmatic people who tend to identify themselves with what they do (doing) rather than who they are (being). Many working people look forward to retirement as a time to do nothing. They focus on a retirement filled with pleasant fantasies. This future orientation blinds them to the reality of God in the present moment. Many persons may feel that retirement, which strips them of their work, causes them to forfeit their identity. Older adults can turn from the hustle and bustle of getting and spending to a more contemplative life. The new freedom from work constraints offers the gift of time, which can be both curse and blessing. No longer driven by work pressures, these new elders pursue a butterfly existence, flitting from one distraction to the next, constantly asking themselves, "What shall I do today?" The new freedom becomes as much work as the job from which they retired.

Just as vacations or sabbaticals offer renewal and refreshment, the freedom of retirement can be a time of spiritual growth. Henry David Thoreau recorded in his *Journal* that "he [or she] enjoys true leisure who has time to improve his [or her] soul's estate." This improvement of the soul's estate includes both quiet contemplation and active involvement. Recall that the early disciples *experienced* the scene of the risen Lord before they ever recorded it. As the writer of First John states, "What we have heard, what we have seen with our eyes, what we have looked at and touched with our hands, concerning the word of life—this life was revealed, and we have seen it and testify to it" (1:1-2).

The Israelites were on the verge of crossing the Jordan and occupying the Promised Land. It was a time of crisis and change as a new generation, disciplined by the desert, stood poised to fulfill its destiny. But some were fearful of the river, others unsure of their new leader Joshua. And God spoke to Joshua, "I hereby command you: Be strong and courageous; do not be frightened or dismayed, for the LORD your God is with you wherever you go" (Josh. 1:9).

Everyone faces transitions and turning points in life, yet the moment comes when it is time to cross the river. But even at these times, when uncertainty and fear of the unknown grip our hearts, we can go forward with the assurance God is with us. As family or work demands relax by virtue of retirement, vacation, or simply reprioritizing, we have an unparalleled opportunity to use the right side of our brains. We provide ourselves time to get in touch with our life stories through remembering by fantasy, intuition—even dreams.

ROLE OF RIVERS IN THE BIBLICAL STORY

You may recall how Jacob came to a moment of truth at the river Jabbok (Gen. 32:22-32). Returning to his childhood home, Jacob's memory of who he had been and how he had deceived his old father, Isaac, and cheated his brother, Esau, closed in on him. Learning that Esau was coming to meet him with four hundred men, Jacob assumed they were bent on revenge. Alone in the night, one came and wrestled with Jacob until daybreak. As the struggle concluded, the one touched Jacob on the hip and wounded him. Jacob must have remembered his dream of a ladder with angels ascending and descending (Gen. 28). In that vision of new life, Jacob heard God say, "Know that I am with you and will keep you ...wherever you go" (28:15). Wounded yet encouraged, Jacob faced Esau, and a new era began.

All of us at some time or other in our life experiences come to the ford of a river where we face moments of transition and change. Like Jacob, we wrestle with former issues we had discarded—old habits, prejudices, and attitudes that stifle our growth—only to discover something new: a new sense of self-worth, new dreams and hopes.

When the armies of Sennacherib descended on Jerusalem in 701 B.C., the city and its citizens were panic-stricken. Psalm 46 reminded the frightened Israelites that "though the earth should change, though the mountains shake in the heart of the sea; though its waters roar and foam, though the mountains tremble with its tumult. There is a river whose streams make glad the city of God" (vss. 2-4). The river symbolized God's life-giving presence. God's presence in the midst of God's people brought security and much-needed help.

We too have known moments of panic and threats to our well-being, along the journey we call life. At times we have felt helpless, doomed to certain defeat and disaster, only to discover the gracious presence of God guiding us through those endless dark nights of the soul.

The prophet of the Exile wrote words of comfort to those who had "received from the Lord's hand double for all [their] sins" (Isa. 40:2) as he likened their trouble to onrushing rivers that threatened to drown them: "When you pass through the waters, I will be with you; and through the rivers, they shall not overwhelm you" (Isa. 43:2). No doubt the prophet was calling into their memory that grace moment when the Egyptian army in pursuit attempted to regain the Hebrew people as slaves by the edge of the water. God delivered the Hebrews. Just as God delivered those ancient people, so God could be with those in exile even if it meant a new crossing of the sea. We see this deliverance from fear in the New Testament when Jesus calmed the waves and the fears of the disciples (Luke 8:22-25).

We all can recall moments when life rushed in upon us and threatened to overwhelm us, memories of painful hours when we wondered if we could survive. Again we made it by God's grace.

It was "by the rivers of Babylon" that God's people sat down and wept when they *remembered* Zion (Ps. 137:1). Broken by their captivity, huddled in silent grief beside a strange river in an even stranger land, they cried, "How could we sing the LORD's song in a foreign land?" (Ps. 137:4). For those in later life today "the rivers of Babylon" may include displacement from home and placement in a retirement community or nursing home. "The rivers of Babylon" may make us feel swept aside after retirement.

At the river Jordan Jesus faced a crucial moment in his ministry (Matt. 3:13-17). At his baptism by John, he finally accepted his vocation as God's servant. In that moment Jesus realized that his mission would not entail political power or spectacular signs. Rather, it would mean being God's suffering servant, whose vulnerable love would lead ultimately to the cross. All of us face moments in our lives when we come to the river of decision. We need to hear God's call for ourselves, whether it be early in life, in our middle years, or even after retirement.

In his novel *A River Runs through It*, writer Norman Maclean vividly describes the sharp angles of Big Blackfoot River in Montana. It runs straight for a while, then turns abruptly, meets boulders, turns sharply, runs smoothly again. He draws this conclusion from the river's course:

> Eventually, all things merge into one, and a river runs through it. The river was cut by the world's great flood and runs over rocks from the basement of time. On some of the rocks are timeless raindrops. Under the rocks are the words, and some of the words are theirs.
> I am haunted by waters.[2]

You are going to take an imaginary journey for the next few minutes. Quietly read the directions and experience each step of the guided meditation.

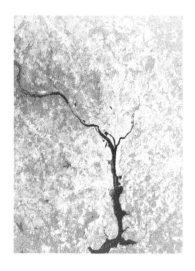

THE RIVER OF LIFE GUIDED MEDITATION

- Your whole life is a river, and you can see it there before you. You can see its beginning; how does it start for you? Is it a spring? Does it come up from a lake? What does that mean to you? *(1 minute)*

- You look down the river, and you see many tributaries, the sources that fed your river in the beginning. You notice what they are and where they come from. You notice the sources of your water, and you understand them. What do they mean to you? *(2 minutes)*

- You remember that God is with you now and throughout your life. You see changes in the direction of your river. What are they? Where do they take you? What does that mean to you? *(1 minute)*

- Where were there changes in the current? *(30 seconds)*

- Where were there changes in the depth of the water? *(30 seconds)*

- Where were there boulders or obstacles in your river? How does the water overcome them? *(2 minutes)*

- In what places is water poured out or drained out to nourish others? *(1 minute)*

- Now notice the mouth of the river. What does it look like? What does that mean to you? *(1 minute)*

- Look again at the whole river. Was it fast and turbulent? slow and meandering? quiet and deep? What do you see now that is important to you? How did you recognize God's grace? *(2 minutes)*

Once you feel you have a good picture of your river, gently and slowly come back to the room, take a piece of paper and pencil, and make a representation of your river. You may choose to make a drawing; you may or may not have notes explaining features of the river; you may have a narrative or some poetry. Represent your river in any way that works for you. You may want to follow up this experience by writing in a journal or talking to a friend.

As you experience the "River of Life" you will discover amazing parallels between the life of the river and your own story. Listen to how some people connected the image of the river with some of their life story:

Dr. Barbara Nagy, a physician, used the river image to describe her amazing adoption of two little Chinese girls, Melia and Anna. "If I had not adopted them, they might not have lived," she said. "So the river of my life has flowed beyond myself into the lives of two young Chinese girls."

A businessman was "downsized" from his job at midlife. He said, "It was as if a great boulder had been placed to stop the flow of the river. But I went right through that experience and found a new career, and life flowed on."

We stood at the river for the final farewell of her husband. He had been cremated, and his wishes were to scatter his ashes in the river. As we watched his ashes disappear into the water, his widow quoted the words of George Matheson's hymn "O Love That Wilt Not Let Me Go":

> *O Love that wilt not let me go,*
> *I rest my weary soul in thee;*
> *I give thee back the life I owe,*
> *That in thine ocean depths its flow*
> *may richer, fuller be.*

The following poem by William Stafford raises significant questions about one's life story.

> *Sometime when the river is ice ask me*
> *mistakes I have made. Ask me whether*
> *what I have done is my life. Others*
> *have come in their slow way into*
> *my thought, and some have tried to help*
> *or to hurt: ask me what difference*
> *their strongest love or hate has made.*

I will listen to what you say.
You and I can turn and look
at the silent river and wait. We know
the current is there, hidden; and there
are comings and goings from miles away
that hold the stillness exactly before us.
What the river says, that is what I say.[3]

What might the poet mean when he writes, "Ask me whether what I have done is my life"?

In what ways is your life hidden, like the river, beneath the ice? Explain.

What do you believe the poet means when he writes, "What the river says, that is what I say"? What does the river say?

Regardless of what story the river of your life might tell, the truth remains that the river of God's life-giving presence is always there. Meditate on the words of the poem "Sometimes" by Geraldine A. Goss.

SOMETIMES

BY GERALDINE A. GOSS

Sometimes,
like a mighty river
that thunders and echoes
through weathered canyon walls,
Your Word floods my soul, Lord,
surging in with power to cleanse away debris.

Sometimes,
like a quiet stream
that meanders, sparkling
through a sun-dappled vale,
Your Word flows gently, Lord,
through my aching heart
to comfort and to heal.

Sometimes,
like a swift, deep current
that rushes to the sea,
Your Living Word flows on
through me to others, Lord,
in leaping, pulsing waves,
and sounds the depths of love.

You may wish to close by reading the following "Prayer of Thanksgiving."

O God, who has written in your eternal word, "For everything there is a time and a season for everything under heaven," we praise you for all seasons of life.

For the springtime, when life bursts in newness and joy; for the innocence of little children with their incessant probing questions; for the awkward honesty of teenagers;

For the summer with its relentless activity, which drives adults to endless achievements and good works; for the warmth of maturing relationships and the assurance that in the midst of life there is an invincible summer;

For the autumn of life, when our feverish rush is tempered by the need to rest and reflect; for its golden richness that speaks of the wisdom and mellowness of older persons;

For the winter, when often all we can do is wait while snow lies on top of the land; yet we remain aware that you are preparing the strong light and warm winds that lead to spring; when we realize that life's end is never far away, yet there is always hope for the resurrection morning.

For all these seasons of life, we praise you, O Ancient of Days. Amen.

CHAPTER FOUR

RECLAIMING CHILDHOOD STORIES

When I was a child, I spoke like a child,
I thought like a child.
—1 CORINTHIANS 13:11

He called a child, whom he put among them,
and said, "Truly I tell you, unless you change and
become like children, you will never enter
the kingdom of heaven."
—MATTHEW 18:2-3

Everyone has, or lives, or is, a story. In the life
review the plot line is not always clear. There are
many subplots, detours, and wildernesses in each
journey. But connections are made; we can
remember pieces of our lives.
—ROY W. FAIRCHILD

*L*uke's story of the boy Jesus in the Temple at the age of twelve (Luke 2:41-52) is the only Gospel story we have of Jesus' boyhood, and at that young age he amazes the learned rabbis with his wisdom and understanding. I have always wondered why Luke did not record more stories of Jesus' boyhood and adolescence. Why are the Gospels so silent about Jesus' growing-up years in Nazareth? We lose sight of him after the birth stories, except for this one story in the Jerusalem temple. The next stories focus on Jesus' baptism by John, Jesus' acceptance of his vocation, and his public ministry. What of those other years? Where was he? What was he doing? We can only speculate.

Apocryphal writings contain incredible stories about Jesus' childhood suggesting that he could make clay sparrows and then bring them to life and that when a schoolmate pushed him roughly in a game, Jesus turned the boy to stone. Though we long for more details of the childhood, we acknowledge the Gospels' concern with Jesus' ministry. And as we think of Jesus' childhood and wonder, we also recall our own childhood.

FOUR AGES OF LIFE

We may think of life in four quarters:

- First Age (birth to age 25)
- Second Age (ages 26–50)
- Third Age (ages 51–75)
- Fourth Age (ages 76–100 and beyond)

During the First Age (birth to age 25), life revolves around family and school. Parents are the central figures, and a child's becoming a responsible individual may depend at first on parental adequacy. Later, teachers and friends become central figures. The First Age is the age of preparation for responsible adulthood.

The Second Age (26–50) is launched when a person begins working, establishes a family, or gains a sense of purpose or mission in life. It is the age of clearly defined roles and responsibilities, a time when commitments are made.

The Third Age (51–75) has witnessed many changes due to the extended life span related to the marvels of medical technology. In this age persons continue to grow and expand horizons, to find redirection of life beyond the working role. The Third Age can become a time of choice with regard to returning talents and gifts to society and the world. It is a time to launch out in new directions, unimpeded by the stress of the workaday world.

The Fourth Age (76–100 and beyond) may be a time marked by the inevitable losses and frailties of age; older persons may face suffering of one kind or another. Yet in the Fourth Age, faith can become preeminent. William Clements sees the fourth quarter of life as a time when "a person's desire and ability to make sense out of their existence, to draw together a meaningful life trajectory is best done."[1]

Childhood memories are an integral part of our present consciousness. Who you are today, your basic personality, your philosophy of life, lie hidden within your earliest childhood memories. While distant, childhood is always a part of us. As full-grown women and men we carry tiny, whimpering children around inside us. Frederick Buechner has written,

> In one sense the past is dead and gone, never to be repeated, over and done with, but in another sense, of course it is not done with at all or at least not done with us. Every person we have ever known, every place we have ever seen, everything that has ever happened to us—it all lives and breathes deep within us somewhere whether we like it or not, and sometimes it doesn't take much to bring it back to the surface in bits and pieces.[2]

We may look at a faded photograph, glance at an old book from our childhood, or visit a childhood neighborhood; and memories flood our minds and hearts. Some people prefer to leave old memories buried in the past. But the only way to discover our real selves is to go back. We go back, not because our family is there, but to find ourselves. We go back because part of us is still there.

CHILDHOOD MEMORIES

Memory is a powerful thing, a wonderful gift—for in remembering we do more than recall past events. In a sense we bring these remembered events into the present and find that they nurture us in the here and now. In the book of Hosea we find these words: "When Israel was a child, I loved him, and out of Egypt I called my son" (11:1). Verses 1-4 of this chapter picture God as a loving parent who teaches little Ephraim to walk and who leads and feeds the Israelites with kindness.

As children we also experience our Egypts, which include fears, insecurities, anxieties and, at times, oppression and bondage. We too have cried to God for deliverance, and God has called us out of our Egypts into freedom and maturity. As we relive our childhood memories, they tell us who we are.

Take a few minutes to picture a house you lived in as a child. Enter each room and get a mental picture of the furniture of that room. Include as many objects as you can remember. Perhaps you may recall some of the smells and sounds of that house. In the space provided take a pencil and draw a house plan of the house you grew up in. Choose a house you remember best before the age of ten. To draw a floor plan, see the house as if you were looking down from above. Picture the rooms, the placement of furniture in the rooms, and the location of windows and doors. Notice important features of the yard.

As you draw the house, memories of things that happened in those rooms will come to mind. Jot down a note below to remind you of an incident or story.

....

If any area of the house brings up painful memories, you do not have to go there. For example, I remembered the door of the manse where my family lived because for one whole year a quarantine sign was tacked to the door. Except for teachers who came from the schools to tutor my siblings and me, we were confined at home and permitted no other contact with the outside world. Many painful memories of that year remain.

In the movie *The Trip to Bountiful*, Carrie Watts makes a sentimental journey to her former home. She softly sings the old hymn, "Come home, come home, Ye who are weary come home" as she returns to Bountiful, Texas. Her memories sustain her during hard times: thoughts of her childhood friend Callie Davis, nights when the moon was full and she'd waken her son Ludie so they could walk in the magical light. She remembers Ludie's favorite song as a child back in the days when "everybody was so poor, but we all got along." Heartbreaking memories return: memories of Rennie Sue and Douglas, her two children who died in infancy and are buried in Bountiful's earth; the poignant memory of the only man she ever really loved but was not permitted to marry. The days are full of memories that sustain her and make her want to go home to Bountiful one more time before she dies.

If you can make such a trip, your returning to the places of birth and childhood will trigger many memories. If that trip is physically impossible, you can go there in your imagination. Or you might contact long-lost friends and reminisce about your old neighborhood.

One of my most powerful childhood memories is of my fascination with Frances Hodgson Burnett's book *The Secret Garden*. The story of Mary

Lennox captivated me. The secret garden that Mary found and its healing power for Colin was a story with which I identified as a child. I too had a secret garden.

Although it has been more than sixty years since I played in my own secret garden, I can still see it in my mind: a secluded place at the back of the manse. Walled off from the rest of the yard, the garden had been overtaken by weeds; but I discovered an open place where I could sit and read. Now I realize that secret garden was my refuge, a place of solace and strength for a small boy who had almost died from pneumonia before he'd had a chance to live.

All of us have childhood places that remain in our memories as favorites, our "secret gardens." To stir your memories of some of these favorite childhood spots, consider some of the following questions:

 What does your favorite place look like?

What story do you associate with your favorite place?

Why do you remember this place so vividly?

What smells and sounds do you associate with this place?

For many persons the most cherished childhood memories are associated with Christmas. Christmas memories often rekindle the magic of childhood. Write your responses to these questions as you think of childhood Christmas celebrations:

What is your earliest memory of Christmas?

What special gifts did you receive or give at this season?

What memorable worship service, pageant, or tradition do you recall?

What do you remember doing at Christmas for someone in need?

FAMILY SECRETS

In his book *Telling Secrets*, Frederick Buechner shares the story of his father's drinking and suicide. Reflecting on this well-kept family secret, he says, "Don't talk, don't trust, and don't feel is supposed to be the unwritten law of families that for one reason or another have gone out of whack."[3] His family, especially his mother, never talked about his father's suicide. Only half a century later did the ten-year-old boy he was at the time of his father's death emerge to tell the story and realize the deeper secret. "Although death ended my father it never really ended my relationship with my father—a secret that I had never so clearly understood before."[4]

One parental script we receive is this: "What you don't know won't hurt you." Some children have been kept in the dark for years about family skeletons rattling in the closet. Yet we may act out the family's dark secrets without living our own lives—as, for example, the effect parental alcoholism has on children on into their own adulthood. Jesus said, "There is nothing hidden, except to be disclosed; nor is anything secret, except to come to light" (Mark 4:22).

One family secret that I learned later in life was that at the age of six, I almost died of pneumonia. The incident occurred before the advent of penicillin, and the doctor advised my parents not to take me to the hospital since I was near death. For years afterward I was a chronic hypochondriac; only later did I realize that that condition resulted in part from my overhearing Dr. Scott's words at the age of six. Doctors and parents need to speak with caution in the presence of sick children, because they hear more than realized. But getting in touch with that family secret was a healthy experience that brought self-understanding and change to my life.

Another family secret that I came to know later in life was the circumstances surrounding my birth. At the hour of my birth, my grandfather G. Campbell Morgan, internationally known British biblical expositor, was preaching a sermon on the subject "The New Birth"—a fact that seemed to mark me for the ministry from the moment of my nativity. Although I did not learn of these circumstances until later in life, they merely reinforced my need to enter the ministry as the oldest son in a British family, carrying on the family tradition. I carried out this script from a false sense of guilt. For years I acted as if I had no alternative vocational possibilities. Unhappy years in the parish ensued. Only through therapy did I extricate myself from this script and become a counselor. When I did return to parish ministry in later years, it was *my choice*, and that was no secret!

 What family secrets have influenced your life?

You may choose to share a secret from your story. Your sharing makes it easier for others to tell a secret or two of their own; through this sharing, we discover what it means to trust another person.

RECLAIMING OUR CHILDHOOD VIEW OF GOD

Merle R. Jordan claims that our family of origin is the microcosm where our relationships with self, others, and God are formed. The rules, beliefs, and scripts we learn in childhood persist into adult life. He says that "deep spiritual transformation may better occur when you have differentiated from your family of origin so that you harbor no ultimate loyalties that would block a total commitment to God in Christ."[5] All of us can be anchored in the views of God we inherit from our families of origin, and we need to pull up these anchors from our past, so we can move forward on a journey that is really ours.

Every child has a mental picture of God. Roberta C. Bondi tells how she outgrew her childish view of God: "There was the Christian God I knew from the Calvinistic Sunday schools and Baptist revivals of my childhood who continued to grip my guilty imagination with threats of love, images of judgment, and demands of belief."[6] Only later in her spiritual journey did she come to realize the gentleness of God, "who especially loved the ones the world despises, and who is always so much more willing than human beings to make allowances for sin, because it is God alone who sees the whole of who we are and who we have been."[7]

From my own childhood I recall my fearful images of God as some cosmic bookkeeper in the sky, damning me forever if I sinned too much. On the other hand I felt drawn to Jesus as the friend of children and the One who loved me regardless of my faults. Certainly the images of God we bring from childhood can narrow our views of God. We may find ourselves locked in to particular ideas, views, traditions, and images.

J. B. Phillips in his book *Your God Is Too Small* claimed that most people have not found "a God big enough for modern needs." He attempted to (1) expose the inadequate conceptions of God and (2) suggest ways in which we can find the real God for ourselves.

Are any of Phillips's inadequate conceptions of God some of your childhood images of God?

- God as a resident police officer

- God as a parental holdover

- God as a grand old man

- God as absolute perfection

- God as heavenly bosom

- God as a perennial grievance

Reflect now on some of your childhood memories of God. Remember church experiences, childhood prayers, and Bible stories. As you recall these memories, think about your current understanding of God. What changes have you experienced in your relationship with God? As you bring a close to your time of reflection, pray aloud the following:

> **Loving God, you intricately wove us in your own image. Though flawed, though moving ever nearer to inevitable death, we know that you mercifully stay with us. Your Holy Spirit continues to form, save, and buoy us on our journey on the river of life, preparing us for sure and sheer transformation at the end.**

From all that would hinder your great will and design for us,

Good Lord, deliver us.

From all that would set generation against generation,

Good Lord, deliver us.

From deafness to truths you speak through each stage of life,

Good Lord, deliver us.

For patience and courage on our trek toward wholeness and unity,

Hear our prayer, Good Lord.

For wisdom to love both baby and oldster in every generation,

Hear our prayer, Good Lord.

For boldness to hold, to heed, to hearten your diverse children,

Hear our prayer, Good Lord.

That we may nurture the infant and the ancient in all of us,

Grant us your vision and strength, O God.

That we may face the completion of our own rebirth with faith, bravery, and the consolation and fellowship of your children of all ages and generations,

Grant us your vision and strength, O God.

Hear us through Christ, who ever treads beside us.

Amen.

FAMILY RELATIONSHIPS, FAMILY STORIES

And [Jesus] replied, "Who are my mother and my brothers?" And looking at those who sat around him, he said, "Here are my mother and my brothers! Whoever does the will of God is my brother and sister and mother."
—MARK 3:33-35

Deciphering family secrets takes us into the heart of the family's mysterious power to impact our lives. I call this journey into the family's secret world soul-searching....It asks us to listen to our family's stories without our previous judgments and our habituated ways of understanding.
—JOHN BRADSHAW

*F*amily stories enrich us. In other times and other cultures, older people told their stories, which became a sort of wisdom-glue that held communities together. The elders became role models of wisdom and strength for the young. Yet today we are separated from our family stories. We move; we divorce; we interact with the Internet instead of with each other. Few people tell the old stories anymore. So we have lost connection with our heritage and with *the* Story that binds us in community.

In remembering life in our family of origin and the stories that often are kept hidden in closets and closed minds, we discover the forces that made us what we are today, helping to put our lives in perspective. As you recalled your childhood, you probably called to mind vivid memories of your first family. Our early family life is a critical key to who we are now. Our parents and other family members were our whole world during those early years. Your individual story is set within a framework of family history of rules, customs, traditions, taboos, and ways of interacting that shape personalities.

In *Telling Secrets* Frederick Buechner wrote, "Who knows what all of us have in us not just of our parents but of their parents before them and so on back beyond any names we know or any faces we would recognize if we came upon their portraits hanging on an antique shop wall?"[1]

As we begin our attempt to remember our stories, recalling early family relationships and events is of utmost importance. Our family gave us our first concept of home; the more we know about our families, the more we know about ourselves. Many of us would prefer to sweep our family history under the rug, but it lives on inside of us. As Monica McGoldrick has expressed it, "Family will inevitably come back to haunt us—in our relationships with our spouses, our children, our friends and even at work."[2]

FAMILY RELATIONSHIPS

In order to remember some of your earliest memories of your family of origin, try this exercise.

- Write the word *family* in the center of the page, and circle it.
- Link your first association to it with a connecting line. Then branch out to other associations.

Let me illustrate this "clustering" exercise by focusing on the word *Father* as my center. My associations would be the following:

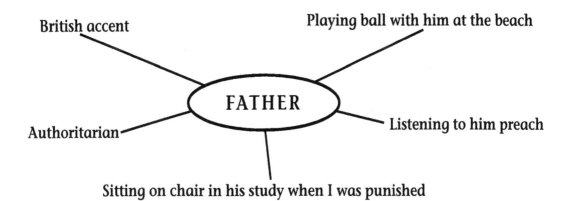

Take a sheet of paper and, with family as your center, draw lines to various associations that you make with that word. After five minutes, pause. Are your associations few or many? pleasant or unpleasant? What does this exercise tell you about your family memories?

Connecting relationships comprise any family system. To understand our childhood families, we need to understand the interactions among family members. Such questions as these are important:

Who held the power in my family?

Who made the decisions?

To whom did I go for comfort and love?

To whom was I closest?

Of whom was I afraid?

What were some family rules?

What stories were told most in my family?

What do these stories reveal about my family?

What stories do I know about my father or mother before they were married?

What stories (that I now know) were suppressed in my family?

Why were they not told?

FAMILY NAMES

The name your family gave you may tell a lot about your family's program or dreams for their child. For example, Benjamin Franklin, the youngest son of Josiah Franklin, was named Benjamin for his uncle and godfather. Franklin was also a "replacement" child, for no fewer than three other sons were lost around the time of his birth. The first, Ebenezer, had drowned unattended in the bath at age two. The next son, Thomas, died a few months later. Josiah, the father's namesake, ran away to sea at age twenty-one. The irony of Benjamin's name was that Uncle Benjamin and Josiah vied for the boy's allegiance, and Ben Franklin became more like his Uncle Benjamin later in life.

 Names given you are significant. Why did your parents give you your name?

How has this name affected your life?

FAMILY ROLES

Family roles are also important. Do you see yourself or any of your siblings acting out the following roles in your early family life? Do you see yourself in more than one role?

The Star or Hero: The one favored by the family for success, giving the family a sense of destiny.

The Caretaker: The child who feels responsible for taking care of the family's pain.

The Clown: The child whose humor and antics become a means of relieving family anxiety.

The Scapegoat: The child who always seems to bear the brunt of shame and is the one most often blamed.

The Lost Child: The child who was unplanned or unwanted.

Explain your role choices:

What patterns or thoughts emerge about your family?

SIBLING RELATIONSHIPS

William B. Oglesby, in his book *Biblical Themes for Pastoral Care*, finds characteristic responses of conforming or rebellion in family relationships. For example, Cain, Esau, and the elder brother in Jesus' parable try to gain approval from the father by acceptable behavior, resenting favor granted to others, especially siblings who don't always do the right thing. Abel, Jacob, and the younger son seek recognition by rebelling.

In the family the conforming child is often perceived as the "family hero" who can do no wrong. He or she is favored by the parents and seems destined for a bright future. On the other hand, the rebellious child is often perceived as "the problem child" who is always doing wrong. Parents often say, "This child will never get it together."

One woman told the group that in her family of origin her brother Fred was the chosen one, the favorite, petted and coddled and scripted for success. Her brother Bill and she were perceived either as "problem children" or "nonpersons." What parallels do you see with these sibling relationships in your family?

James Redfield, in his book *The Celestine Vision,* identifies four control dramas that begin in childhood and continue throughout life. The Poor Me or the Victim seeks to win attention through the manipulation of sympathy and the creation of guilt trips for others. Aloof Persons create a mysterious aura around themselves that distances them from others. The Interrogator uses criticism and has to monitor other persons and situations to be in constant control. The Intimidator wins attention by creating an environment in which others feel so threatened they focus totally on him or her. Often parents operate from control dramas. For example, an Aloof parent would be distant; a Poor Me parent would constantly blame or shame the child, while an Intimidator would create a constant climate of fear.

 Which of these dramas do you recognize in your family of origin? Identify them:

The Poor Me

The Aloof

The Interrogator

The Intimidator

FAMILY STORIES

Michael E. Williams writes that "the telling of stories is woven into the fabric of our lives....Story reminds us to which communities we belong. Family stories tell us that we are part of a community related by blood."[3]

Today a new situation confronts us, a situation that often precludes our knowing family stories. Before World War II, three generations of many American families lived in the same town. The family told its saga around the dinner table. How well I recall hearing stories about life on the farm in Iowa from my aged grandmother who lived with us.

Now three generations may live in different states or countries. Unless we preserve and share the family stories with them, they will never hear them. Is it any wonder, then, that the prophet Isaiah counseled the Israelites, "Look to the rock from which you were hewn, and to the quarry from which you were dug. Look to Abraham your father and to Sarah who bore you" (Isa. 51:1-2). As we get in touch with our family stories, we discover our own story in a new light.

Older members of a family are storytellers, the wisdom keepers of the family. They want to pass on the family history from one generation to the next. Their stories offer a sense of continuity. They transmit knowledge, values, and faith between generations. In telling the stories, older people gain a sense of pride and integrity about their lives as they pass their experience on to future generations.

In the summer of 1999 my brother and I revisited an old family home, Faerholm in Winona Lake, Indiana. It was here that our grandfather, Milford Hall Lyon, an associate of the evangelist Billy Sunday, lived with his family. In the garden of that same house our parents were married in 1923. As we stood on the porch of that old home, memories of the past flooded our minds. We began saying, "Do you remember when...," and we retold stories from our past.

We remembered the Lyon family's villains and heroes. Uncle Merle was the black sheep because he had divorced his wife. Aunt Ruth's story was "kept in the closet" because mental illness in those days was a taboo subject. And Uncle Art was the family jokester and oddball.

So we are born, not just into our family, but also into our families' stories, which both nourish and handicap us. And when we die, the stories of our lives become part of the family tradition.

Recently my family of origin gathered at a seashore spot where we once had summered as children. Many memories returned as we visited houses where we stayed as a family and places we enjoyed during those summers. The past lived again as we walked the endless beaches and remembered seeing wrecked ships and the ever-present lighthouse of Cape May, New Jersey.

One of my sisters reminded us of an incredible story from our childhood in the manse. When our grandfather went to England, he left his parrot, George Rats, Esquire, in the manse. My parents were entertaining the Session one evening at a formal dinner, and the parrot was sequestered in his cage. The Session in those days was a collection of austere, serious old men. My parents were doing their utmost to make this a solemn dinner. Someone said the word *Session*, whereupon George Rats squawked, "The Session can just go to hell!" Our parents were horrified, but the preacher's kids behind closed doors almost died laughing.

 What family stories do you recall now?

 A FAMILY STORY

Read the story in Luke 15:11-32, which centers on family relationships. After reading, consider some of the following questions:

- *Which of the two sons' stories most resembled your childhood? Were you more like the younger son, rebelling to gain recognition; or the older son, who tried to earn love by dutiful, acceptable behavior?*

- *With whom in the story do you identify right now?*

- *Did you experience unconditional love from your parents as both sons did from the father?*

You might also want to reflect on Henri J. M. Nouwen's words about the father's love:

> There is no doubt...about the father's heart. His heart goes out to both of his sons; he loves them both; he hopes to see them together as brothers around the same table; he wants them to experience that, different as they are, they belong to the same household and are children of the same father.[4]

RECONNECTING WITH YOUR FAMILY

The heart of this story of the prodigal son is the final reunion. The wayward son has come home and is reunited with his father. His father's unconditional acceptance has paved the way, and the prodigal feels no need to defend himself or explain his behavior. Gregory Bateson tells the following powerful story:

> There is a famous story about a Chinese master painting a landscape. Just as he is nearly finished, a drop of ink falls on the white scroll, and the disciples standing around him gasp, believing the scroll is ruined. Without hesitating the master takes the finest of hair brushes and, using the tiny glob of ink already fallen, paints a fly hovering in the foreground of the landscape.[5]

Reconnecting with your family may well mean opening old wounds and rekindling some bitter memories. But there is grace and meaning even in these experiences. Some of us may not want to know who our ancestors were. We feel no connection, or perhaps we even fear the connection. But to know our roots is to have our identities intact and to know from whom we have come—though not their whole stories, to be sure, for no human being really knows another.

Family stories *are* important, for they remind us that though our lifetimes are short, every person along our family line has been a channel through which our existence had to pass. And one day we too will form part of the continuum as our individual stories are woven into the fabric of generations.

Close your time of thought and reflection by praying "A Litany for the Generations," written by Dwyn M. Mounger:

Loving God, we thank you that at the dawn of time you said, "It is not good that the man should be alone," so you set the solitary in families.

We pause now to thank you for our families of origin, for the loving mystery of that circle of hovering presence that surrounded us in our childhood.

We confess we are too prone to blame persons in our family of origin for our problems and too blind to realize how they tried to love us.

We pause now to remember those in our families who have died, whom we have loved long since and lost awhile. We remember them by name, _____, and bless their memory.

O God of all the human family, from whom every family in heaven and on earth takes its name, your love sustains us now in our family life. As we face the most basic tasks and deal with complicated emotions, be our guardian, guide, and stay.

If it be your will that we care for family members, help us wrestle with the roller-coaster emotions that go hand in hand with caring. Replace anger with compassion, guilt with gratitude, distress with patience, and despair with hope.

And Lord, if it be your will that we receive the care of family members, encourage us to be cheerful, upbeat recipients of that care, seasoning every day with a sense of humor.

As you have taught us to do unto others as we want done unto us, create in us genuine compassion for family members who are difficult, stubborn, or unforgiving.

We remember family members distanced from us either physically or emotionally. Even when we cannot change their attitudes, grant us serenity to accept what cannot be changed and help us to remember them in prayer.

We give you heartfelt thanks for your blessed family of faith, which transcends all human ties and binds us together in faith. Amen.

6

STORIES
CONNECT
GENERATIONS

We will tell to the coming generation
the glorious deeds of the Lord,
and his might, and the wonders that he has done...
that the next generation might know them,
the children yet unborn,
and rise up and tell them to their children.
—Psalm 78:4b, 6

No generation's needs are truly met. Segregated
societies are intellectually stagnant
and emotionally poisoned. Only when all ages
are welcome into the great hoop of life
can a culture be a healthy one.
—Mary Pipher

*O*ne of the most well-kept stories of my family finally came to light. Hushed up for years by the family, it seems half truth and half myth. In 1927 my aunt Ruth Lyon was hospitalized for schizophrenia. The family story was that her puritanical father refused to allow her to marry a man "who had too many vices," so she fled to Florida. Later she was incarcerated in a mental hospital in Chicago for twenty-five years.

In 1952 Aunt Ruth was the second person in the United States to be put on chlorpromazine (Thorazine). She snapped out of her illness, went to graduate school, and taught school until she retired. Following her retirement she traced her family roots back to England and Scotland. Her tireless search for her family's history was in large measure a search to find herself, to connect with her story. Aunt Ruth became the family historian.

John O'Donohue says that "At a deeper level, a family is an incredible intertwining of multiple streams of ancestry, memory, shadow, and light....Though each family is a set of new individuals, ancient relics and residues seep through from past generations. Except for our parents and grandparents, our ancestors have vanished. Yet ultimately and proximately, it is the ancestors who call us here. We belong to their lifeline."[1]

People have always been intrigued by their ancestors. Just consider the many references to family links between people of different generations in the Bible. Jesus' genealogy is recorded in Luke and Matthew. Matthew's genealogy (Matt. 1:18-25) lists forty-two generations from Abraham to Joseph and states that Jesus' line contains such nefarious characters as Rahab, Tamar, and Bathsheba. In his speech before the Jewish Sanhedrin, Stephen recounts the history of the Hebrew people and mentions his ancestors many times (Acts 7).

It is important to know our family history, to connect across generations. We carry within us not only our family of origin but the dead generations, passed on to the future through our children.

THE SEGREGATION OF GENERATIONS

Our mobile, technological society has isolated generations. Families no longer interact across generations but are distanced and seldom together. Formerly members of several generations lived in close proximity to one another, knew and supported one another. It was not uncommon for people to live their entire lives in the same community; three or even four generations of a family would live in the same region.

Change is now the norm. Our mobile lifestyle has spread families across the country and, with increasing frequency, across the oceans. Now families rush from one activity to another; the days when family members lingered after the meal to share stories are almost extinct. We may talk "at" each other, but when was the last time we really listened to each other's stories? Our children spend a disproportionate amount of time being entertained or preoccupied by surfing the Net and computer games. Despite this marvelous progress in communication technology, our world has grown increasingly less personal. Jack Maguire, in his book *The Power of Personal Storytelling*, relates the following story:

> The storyteller Ron Evans talks about a friend who visited an African village shortly after the first television set was introduced there. He learned from one of the villagers that they adored this modern marvel for two weeks, hovering around it whenever they could spare the time, but one by one they gradually abandoned it. When he asked his informer why, he was told, "Oh, we don't need it. We have the storyteller."
>
> "But don't you think the television knows many stories?" Evans's friend asked.
>
> "Oh, yes," the villager replied. "The television knows many stories, but the storyteller knows me."[2]

Activities that once pulled families together—caring for frail elders, minding small children, and telling family stories—are things of the past. Grandparents often live in distant states and see grandchildren infrequently and for short visits. While at one time grandparents were valued for their wisdom and experience, distance and distractions have meant that that role has been lost. Also, the rising number of single-parent families means that children are frequently estranged from one side of the family and know little about an important part of their heritage.

In her classic book *Another Country*, Mary Pipher says,

We are seeing signs of this disintegration in our culture. Children watch television instead of hearing stories….Parents feel isolated and overwhelmed, and elders go days without speaking to anyone. No generation's needs are truly met….Only when all ages are welcome into the great hoop of life can a culture be a healthy one.[3]

THE IMPORTANCE OF FAMILY HISTORY

When we hear any family story or a secret about a grandparent or parent, our own lives suddenly become clearer to us. We are born not just into a family but into our family's stories, which remain a part of us.

 In the space below, jot down some of the important stories or secrets you have learned from your family history.

GENOGRAMS HELP IDENTIFY FAMILY ROLES

In the 1970s Dr. Murray Bowen invented the concept of genogram as part of his family systems model. The genogram is a schematic diagram of the family's multigenerational relationships and patterns. Typically genograms show three generations, listing names, births, marriages, and death dates. A variety of lines indicates relationships such as estranged, close, and very close relationships.

Monica McGoldrick says genograms contain "three types of family information:

1. the basic facts, such as who is in the family, the dates of their births, marriages, moves, illnesses, deaths;

2. information regarding the primary characteristics and level of functioning of different family members, such as education, occupation, psychological and physical health, outstanding attributes, talents, successes, and failures; and

3. relationship patterns in the family—closeness, conflict, or cutoff."[4]

Using symbols and notations, one can chart patterns that repeat themselves through several generations. Dates of births, deaths, and marriages can be noted, as well as whether relationships were close or conflictual.

Some of the universal symbols are these:

☐ = male
○ = female
⊠ ⊗ = deceased
ⓐ = adopted child

Relationships are indicated by connecting lines:

└___┘ = married
└........┘ = unmarried
└_#_┘ = divorced

Connections between two people:

═══ = close
⋀⋀⋀ = conflicted

EXAMPLE OF A GENOGRAM

Maternal Grandparents

      Effie (1870–1964)   m. 1889   Milford (1868–1946)

Fraternal Grandparents

      Campbell (1863–1945)   m. 1888   Annie (1865–1946)

Parents

      Howard (1901–1979) m. 1921 Margaret (1901–1967)

You

      Richard (1929–   Marian (1930–

           m. 1952 / dv. 1975

                       Alice Ann (1934–

       m. 1978

 On a separate piece of paper you may wish to construct a genogram of three generations in your family.

FIVE GENERATIONAL TYPES

It is important to distinguish and describe five generations that have lived since 1901 and to understand each generation's perspective. Only then can we begin to understand and accept the real differences that exist between generations.

THE CIVICS (Veterans; ages 75–100, born between 1901 and 1926)

The oldest generation still living, its members developed their approach to the world during the Depression and World War II and represent what Tom Brokaw calls "The Greatest Generation." They are patriotic, trust-worthy, and have a heritage of sacrifice for the common good. They have a black-and-white approach to right and wrong; their main values are loyalty, responsibility, and teamwork. Having created the largest genera-tion of babies in American history, they are now past their seventies and living healthier, longer lives than their parents did. Anna and Simeon, two aged persons whose lives typify faithfulness and duty, represent bib-lical examples of the Civic Generation.

THE ADAPTIVES (Silent Generation; ages 56–74, born between 1927 and 1944)

Children of the Civics, the Adaptives grew up in a world of war and eco-nomic deprivation. They well remember gas rationing, air raid blackouts, and World War II stories. They came of age too late to fight in World War II and believe in a strong family focus. Adaptives created the corporate sys-tem, expanded the American myth, and dominated the helping profes-sions. They are the quiet mediators, detesting conflict and seeking to atone for what they think has been failure with their Boomer children. Isaac, a quiet man and a link between the two generations of Abraham and Jacob, represents a biblical example of the Adaptive or Silent Generation.

THE BOOMERS (Ages 37–55, born between 1945 and 1964)

The Boomers were born in an age of abundance and cultural change. Computers and the driven schedules of two-career families have shaped their work world. They are idealistic in their values but also intensely self-immersed. They are the Prodigal Generation that rejected or challenged traditional institutions and cultural norms. Born into a TV world, they came of age in an era that saw their leaders gunned down. Women of the Boomer generation surged into leadership, and many joined the exodus from the institutional church. Also known as the Powerhouse Generation, they will occupy center stage for some time. The prodigal son in Jesus' parable who resists his father's authority and seeks new experiences in a far country is a biblical model for this generation.

THE GENERATION 13ERS (Gen X, Diverse Generation; ages 19–36, born between 1965 and 1982)

This generation's formative years were colored by Watergate, the AIDS epidemic, super inflation, and divorce. This is the first generation to experience the technological revolution, and its members are pragmatic and skeptical. Gen Xers relate well to Civics but have difficulty relating to the Boomers with whom they have a love/hate relationship. Yet they are concerned with the family and have a strong social passion. Ruth, who cared for her mother-in-law Naomi, is a biblical witness of this generation.

THE MILLENNIALS (Ages infancy to 18, born between 1983 and 2001)

The millennials came of age at the end of the Cold War. Glued to the Internet, they don't remember life before computers or VCRs. Theirs is a world marked by Pokémon and the Harry Potter fantasies. They are also called "Echo Boomers" since they are largely children of the Baby Boomers. They express interest in community affairs and offer promise of becoming strong public servants. Samuel, the boy in the temple, is a biblical prototype of this generation.

It is possible to color code the generations. As you sketch out your family's generations, consider color-coding each one; notice the beauty of the colors as they intermingle:

Gold: The Saints (all who have lived and died before 1901)
Blue: Civics
Orange: Adaptives
Purple: Boomers
Red: Generation 13ers
Green: The Millennials
White: Unborn generations

William Strauss and Neil Howe invite us to see the generations on one long railroad track, with birth the place of origin and death the destination.[5] Along the way are Life Stations from childhood to old age. They identity four generations: youth coming of age, rising adults reaching midlife, midlifers reaching elderhood, and elders reaching advanced older age. Picture a series of generational trains, all heading down the track at varying times. While the Civic train moves from one station to the next, other generational trains roll down the same track, stopping at life stations along the way. At the midlife station, the Silent Generation boards its train. The next train pulls into the coming-of-age station, and rising adults climb aboard the Boomer Generation train. Youth coming of age board the Generation 13 train, while children board the Millennial train. Picture yourself at the station, watching the trains come and go. What characteristics of each generation can you perceive as a particular generation's train passes by. Is the train noisy, silent? Are the shades drawn for privacy, rest? Does the train bear banners? What do they say? What does your generation's train look like?

STORIES FROM ACROSS THE GENERATIONS

Going through my files a few years ago, I discovered an old letter from my grandfather, G. Campbell Morgan, written from London during World War II. "London is going through a tremendous ordeal," he wrote. "I have not been in bed for six weeks. Westminster Chapel has been hit three times, which means we could not hold the service there. The streets look like charred ruins, but we carry on." Sixty years later this story remains a legacy of faith, that my grandfather's commitment to the church was more important than his own security.

 Grandparents are family historians. They are the keepers of the collective memories, the repositories of stories, and the connecting link between generations.

What are some stories you heard about your grandparents?

If you want to preserve your family's heritage, you must commit to memory all the stories you know. Telling them over and over again will anchor them in your memory. Then you need to record these stories for future generations.

LEAVING AN ETHICAL WILL

Judaism supports a tradition of writing an "ethical will."[6] Along with leaving others our money and possessions, we might also like to pass on the values and insights that have guided us through the years. Below is an example of an ethical will outline:

OPENING
> I write this to you, my ...
> In order to ...

THE FAMILY
> 1. My parents, siblings, antecedents were/are...
> 2. Events that helped shape our family...

RELIGIOUS OBSERVANCES, INSIGHTS
> 1. The ritual(s) of most meaning to me...
> 2. Specific teachings from values, spiritual or religious
>   source(s) that move me most...

PERSONAL HISTORY
> 1. People who strongly influenced my life...
> 2. Events which helped shape my life...

ETHICAL IDEALS AND PRACTICES
> 1. Ideals that found expression in my life...
> 2. I would like to suggest to you the following...

CLOSING
> 1. My ardent wishes for you...
> 2. May the Almighty...

FAITH STORIES CONNECT GENERATIONS

Remember that the Bible is full of faith-filled interactions between generations. Moses reminds the Israelites that when the children ask, "What do you mean by this observance?" the parents shall say, "It is the passover sacrifice to the Lord" (Exod. 12:26-27). The boy Samuel ministers to the Lord under the aged priest Eli (1 Sam. 3:1). Luke tells how a young woman discovers she is pregnant and hurries to the house of her aunt (older relative), where she finds refuge, acceptance, and encouragement from a wise female mentor (1:39-56). A bright twelve-year-old is drawn into adult discussion of faith with learned elders of the synagogue (Luke 2:41-52).

Kathleen Fischer writes, "One of the most important contributions older persons make to a Christian community is the sharing of their stories of faith. As bearers of living tradition, they know stages of the Christian journey not yet experienced by the young....The sharing of stories can unify persons across generations....In stories we discover our common faith journey."[7]

The stories of our families in every generation unite us far more than shared chromosomes. Stories are thicker than blood. Somewhere along the way we have lost the art of sharing family stories within our daily lives. But we must regain this art if we are to preserve stories for coming generations. Generations need to connect across the years. If we do not preserve the stories of our families, our faith legacies, how will future generations know them? By snapshots in faded albums? Or contents of a NASA capsule? Only as we remember and preserve the faith stories of our families will future generations know where they have been (even before they were born), where they are, and where they are going.

Nancy Yost expresses the deep connection of generations in her poem, "The Last Spring of My Grandmother."

The last spring of my grandmother
was the first spring of my grandson.
I watch as they regard one another,
she whose eyes saw so much,
he whose eyes so lately opened.

On his christening day
she holds him,
and he, in return,
as if by covenant,
clutches her finger
in his small fist,
trusting,
and giving the gift
only the very young
and the very old can give—
total acceptance.
Each of them declaring,
in their dependency,
their independence,
in this first and final spring.

LITANY OF THANKSGIVING FOR THE GENERATIONS

Leader: Lord, you have been our dwelling place in *all* generations.

People: Yes, your Word says that "One generation shall commend thy works to another and set forth thy mighty deeds."

Millennial: We thank you for the wisdom and experience of older generations. Like the elders of old, they have paved the way for us and made smooth some of the rough places in life. Grant that we may listen to our elders so that the next generation will already know what it is taking us so long to learn.

Civic: We give thanks for young people, for their vision and concern, for their strong bodies that sway in the dance of life. Help us to learn from them to live life to the fullest, seize the moment, and not waste time with trivialities.

Adaptive: We thank you for the blessings that our fathers and mothers bestowed on us. Most especially we praise the sacrifice and courage of our fathers who fought in World War II to preserve our freedom, and the perseverance of our mothers who kept the home fires burning.

Gen Xer: We praise you, O God, for the Boomers, whose struggles for civil rights and justice made it easier for us. In an age of abundance and change they taught us to look within for peace and to cherish simple things that do not change.

Boomer: For the generation that followed us, we give thanks. We even praise you for the challenges they gave us and for the ways in which they made us look at ourselves.

BENEDICTION (PRAYED BY ALL)

Now to God who by the power at work within us is able to do far more abundantly than all we ask or think, to God be glory in the church, and through Christ Jesus to *all* generations. Amen.

FACING
LIFE'S
TRANSITIONS

There is a time for everything, and a season for every activity under heaven: a time to be born and a time to die, a time to tear down and a time to build,... a time to mourn and a time to dance,... a time to search and a time to give up,... a time to tear and a time to mend.
—ECCLESIASTES 3:1-7, NIV

In every person's life, there are crucial points that, from that moment onward, alter the course of his or her life....Looking back, you can see that this was a turning point in your life, that the way you responded to that crisis defined who you are.
—ROBERT U. AKERET

*T*hey sat in a circle listening to stories about life transitions. The road less traveled beckoned to all of them, leaving them wondering what might happen if they took a new direction.

One of the participants had been downsized at work, replaced by a more submissive editor who responded to corporate demands. Another had suddenly become a widow after her athletic husband had collapsed and died of a coronary after running. Two women were struggling to move beyond painful divorces. One said she felt like "a package that had never been opened," while the other described her life as a violent earthquake. One man said he was forced to retire and that the handshakes of the retirement party felt like "golden handcuffs."

For all these people, change was in the air. Transitions had become a way of life.

As I look back at my own life, I recall many crises and transitions. Two stand out. A painful divorce wrenched me from my former life and hurled me like a newborn babe into an existence far less charted than I had ever known. Single life was a crazy time, a strange yo-yo life between relief and despair. I felt like the early Christians, trapped in a gray limbo between a past that had ended and a future that was yet unknown. It was only later that I realized that my "fall from grace" tempered me to be more compassionate to others who had failed.

The second major crisis came with a serious illness that almost ended my life. I will always wonder how close I came to that other shore. Those days and nights when life came to the edge of the precipice will always remain a part of my story. Like Jonah, I crawled out of the belly of despair to be given a second chance at life by the grace of God. Both experiences, however painful, were not disasters but turning points that sensitized me to others' suffering and loneliness.

LIFE'S TURNING POINTS AND TRANSITIONS
A New Image of Life

One of my vivid childhood memories is of riding the merry-go-round at the seashore park. You would think that five rides on a merry-go-round were enough, but I kept begging my parents for "just one more ride."

Finally I stated, "I want to live on the merry-go-round." At times life is like a merry-go-round, but the roller-coaster life is more challenging and interesting. As we review our ups and downs, we gain a greater sense of self-worth and God's gracious providence. We may take one step forward and two back, but somehow we move through these ups and downs ever onward. That is the biblical model of growing older; it is never a matter of going forward or backward but of going onward. We never arrive; we are always on the way, always becoming.

Paul W. Pruyser points out that many people still hold to an "iconic illusion" about life. They view growth as a low-high-low transition; life starts out low, builds to a peak, and then declines. Our society mirrors this view in its hackneyed statements: "Over the hill," "Life goes downhill after forty," or "He's been put out to pasture." Pruyser argues that if we take into account the gains of older life, without denying the losses, "life seems no longer to fit the iconic illusion of low-high-low sequence. A new image shapes up; it is as if someone put a bouquet of flowers in the right-hand vase that stands on the Victorian mantelpiece. It has the power to distract our gaze from the dominance of the clock in the middle."[1]

The new image means that life *always* has its ups and downs; life always has its twists and turns. This view makes us realize that life is never living upward or downward, but always forward as long as we live. When asked which was his best painting, Picasso replied, "The next one!"

So life is not

but

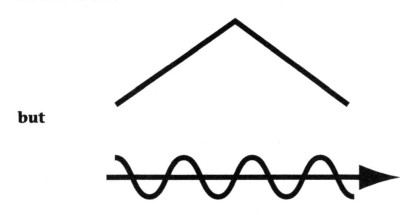

We know that we are on a pilgrimage from birth to death, a zig-zagging route filled with twists and turns. In a movie from a few years back, the matriarch of a family spends much of the film silently observing the struggles of her grandchildren. Her advice reflects her own life review, in which she likens some lives to a roller coaster and others to a merry-go-round.

MIDLIFE TRANSITIONS

Life brings its turning points and transitions. For some they come at midlife. We sense that time is passing away; we begin to count the years from the end rather than the beginning. It is "a time of small deaths," not the least of which is the realization that we will not fulfill our dreams of earlier years. Carl Jung warned of an "ambush" at midlife if we are not prepared for the changes:

> Instead of looking forward, one looks backward...one begins to take stock, to see how his [or her] life has developed up to this point. The real motivations are sought and the real discoveries are made....But these insights do not come to him [or her] easily; they are gained only through the severest shocks.[2]

At midlife, confronted with our finitude and aware of our values, we realize a glaring discrepancy between what we wanted or expected from life and what we now believe is important. Some of us are unhappy about some of the choices we've made over the years, whether it is a career path not taken or a relationship allowed to lapse. Our awareness at midlife of some of these regrets, makes it possible to take new action to undo some of our past mistakes.

TAKING STOCK AT MIDLIFE

Think about these questions as you take stock if you are in midlife:

1. Did I make the right choice about my career in earlier life?
2. Are my present values in conflict with my lifestyle?
3. Did I take enough risks in life?
4. Did I marry too early?
5. Is my marriage [or single life] really fulfilling?
6. Is my relationship with my parents what it could be?

7. Do my beliefs "hold" at this stage of life?

8. Am I satisfied with the level of my education?

9. Have I spent enough time with good friends?

10. If I knew then what I know now, would I have made different decisions about important choices?

LATE LIFE TRANSITIONS

Due to the fact that people are living longer, we face new transitions and turning points in later life that did not exist in earlier times. At retirement a person faces the challenge of what to be in these bonus years. For some people it is a time of extended leisure. For others it is "rise early, work late," so they continue working until health fails. Still others seem to find a creative balance between meaningful work and creative rest. Some will start new careers for pleasure, while others, especially women and minorities, will continue to work for financial reasons.

TAKING STOCK AT RETIREMENT

Think about these questions as you take stock in your retirement years.

1. Do I want to consider part-time work or enjoy some well-deserved leisure time?

2. Would I prefer to maintain my working "busy-ness" or find a balance among work, leisure, and volunteerism?

3. Would I rather devote more time to my grandchildren or my own interests?

4. What will life be like if loss of health or financial constraints do not allow unlimited travel?

5. Do I prefer to make my own plans when I can no longer stay in my own home or depend on my children for this decision?

6. If I do have to downsize to move to a smaller apartment, what things do I need to keep? to give away?

7. If my spouse dies, would I rather stay by myself, either in my home or in an assisted living facility, or live with my children?

LIFE'S TURNING POINTS

All of us, at any stage of life, come to turning points. In retrospect, we look at our life story and recognize moments when we took one path and not the other, and sometimes it *was* "the road less traveled."

Erik Erikson says that crises are turning points that offer critical possibilities. Hence, a turning point can be a variety of things: getting married or divorced, changing jobs or losing a job, having a baby, moving to another town, feeling God's presence in answered prayer, expressing anger about the loss of a loved one, facing a serious illness. Every turning point involves a major transition.

These major turning points—large or small—affect the rest of our lives. William Bridges described three stages in life's transitions: (1) endings followed by (2) a neutral zone, the time between the old life and the new, and (3) a new beginning.[3] One needs time to grieve the loss and struggle through the unknown zone before new beginnings can happen.

This pattern of stages repeats itself. Just when we feel settled, transitions and relocations shatter our security and force us to find new beginnings. All transitions follow a similar cycle, taking us from endings, through emptiness and darkness, to fresh life and new beginnings. This movement reminds us of the cyclical nature of life: the changing seasons, the ebb and flow of the ocean tides, the waxing and waning of the moon. Faith demands that we face the endings, the in-between time, and the emergence of something new with courage and hope.

I well recall the trapeze artists at the circus, swinging on their trapezes high above me in the dome of the circus tent. They had to let go of one trapeze just at the right moment, hovering in the void before catching hold of the other trapeze. It seems as if life is like that: There is always a place to leave and a new place to find.

William Bridges used the biblical story of Moses to explain this three-part cycle. In the first stage, Moses denied the call to lead his people out of Egypt toward freedom. Then Bridges described an interim stage of hesitation and vacillation as the "plague period" when nothing went right for Pharaoh or the Israelites. Only after these stages did Moses and the Israelites experience the Exodus and their new beginning.[4]

Paul experienced a cataclysmic change in his life after the Damascus road experience. He had been hell-bent in his zeal for the traditions of his religion, even murdering followers of Jesus. But he reached the turning point on the road to Damascus, where he gave up that "religion" and found faith as a follower of Christ.

 The Bible cites numerous examples of transitions in people's lives. See if you can connect with any of these transitions.

THE STORY	MY STORY
Abraham's decision to leave his comfortable life for a venture of faith.	
Jacob's wrestling with God over his past life and future plans.	
Moses' living in a wilderness of no identity (nonperson) before God's call to mission.	
Ruth's choosing to forego her own comfort to care for an aging mother-in-law.	
Isaiah's finding the presence of God in a moment of great personal loss.	
Jesus' wrestling with the will of God and deciding to accept the pain of that call upon his life.	
Paul's giving up his former identity for a wilderness experience of being a nobody before discovering his true self.	

Recall the road map you drew when working with chapter 2. Think now of bends in the road, turning points where you had to make a clear decision between two paths. The transitions might involve career choices, marriage issues, geographical moves, illness, and so forth. You may wish to record these turning points or draw them on your road map of life. Keep in mind some of the following questions as you reflect on these turning points:

- When did this turning point occur?

- Who were the significant people involved—parents? spouse? children? yourself alone?

- What were your feelings and emotions at that time?

- How do you now view this turning point in your life? (Perhaps an event that seemed disastrous later became a redemptive experience and vice versa.) How would your decision differ if you came to this turning point today?

- How did this turning point change your life? How would your life have been different if it had not occurred?

Another paradigm for these transitions in life is as follows:

Relinquishment —> Trust —> Transformation

Every transition begins with an ending. We have to let go of the old before we can realize the new. Letting go is hard; often we second-guess ourselves and wonder if we've made the right decision. When we have relinquished the past, then we are thrown into an unknown time where we have to live by trust. It is as if we have launched out from a riverside dock to cross to a landing on the opposite shore—only to discover midstream that the landing is not yet in sight. When we look back to the other shore, we see that dock we've left behind is nowhere in sight either. We find ourselves stranded in midstream.

William Bridges warns that too many people rush through this stage without experiencing the meaning of the void: "We try to find ways of replacing these missing elements as quickly as possible. The neutral zone is...a temporary state of loss to be endured."[5] So people who have lost jobs rush into new employment without taking time to process the change; persons who have lost spouses jump into new relationships without processing their grief. Retired persons fill their days with busyness to cover the void in their lives, without taking time to experience the emptiness.

Linda fled a twenty-year marriage to pursue her career. Later, reflecting on this devastating change in her life, she likened her life to being in a wheelchair, in a place without points of access:

> I sit in my wheelchair watching the world go by. My mobility is now limited....Invisible handicaps are the most devastating kind, and I know my rehabilitation has been painful; the first steps so uncertain that others have had to pick me up when I sped down ramps. My wheelchair is not chrome and steel but the stigma of my divorce. My methods of survival are not tried but true. But I'm using sunsets, roses, and rainbows. I'm starting over.

 Can you relate any experiences where crises forced you to reappraise your life and begin over?

Steve Eason shared a story from his earlier life. At the age of nineteen, he experienced what he called "The Fall of 1972." He remembered attending a play about Galileo's life as a requirement for a physics class. He heard how Galileo argued that the earth was not the center of the universe; the sun at the center displaced and dethroned us. Steve recorded in his journal the following words:

> It was as if someone or something blew away the fog from over my brain. It was as if something straightened me up in my chair, called me to attention, opened my ears, connected the wires between my head and my heart for the first time. I was alive and

never had been so before....I knew in that moment, I knew with all my being...that I lived my life as if I were at the center of the universe. I knew that I must step aside...and that there was something else at the center of my life, and it wasn't me....I didn't have to hold the universe up! There was something in the center of all of life which allowed me, along with all others, to rotate around its force, to be nourished by it. It was the Son.

Years later, as Steve reflected on this life-changing experience, he recognized two truths. The seeds planted by his parents had come to fruition with the aid of God. And God's spirit—outside of human intent and agenda—had interrupted his life. As he wrote, "I was taught in almost the flash of a moment a system of theology that might take years to unpack." Steve is now a Presbyterian pastor. As he thinks back on that event, he says,

Sometimes I fantasize about doing other things, of being free from the church. Sometimes I dream about having another life—one I never had as an adult. Sometimes I long to be released from the burden of pastoral care—the hospital, the funeral home, the broken marriage, the wayward child. Then I remember the Fall of 1972—the fall from the center—a fall into the arms of God.

George, in his late forties, experienced many successes in his career, seemed to have a healthy marriage, and lived in a nice suburban area. His main interests were making money and playing golf and tennis. Suddenly his oldest son dropped out of medical school and returned home with no ambitions. George began to question his own values for the first time. Bored with his life despite his image at work and in the community, George became depressed and restless. He wondered, *Is this all there is*? He began a midlife journey, a new life story.

 For many in the middle years, their life story may take a different direction. Can you recall or think of such experiences in your life story?

STEPPING-STONES

Even in the middle years we look back to discern the pattern of our lives. On the stepping-stones below record landmark events, one event per stone. Then go stone by stone, pausing to consider the recorded event. Think about your perception of God at the time, as well as what you learned about life and faith from that event.

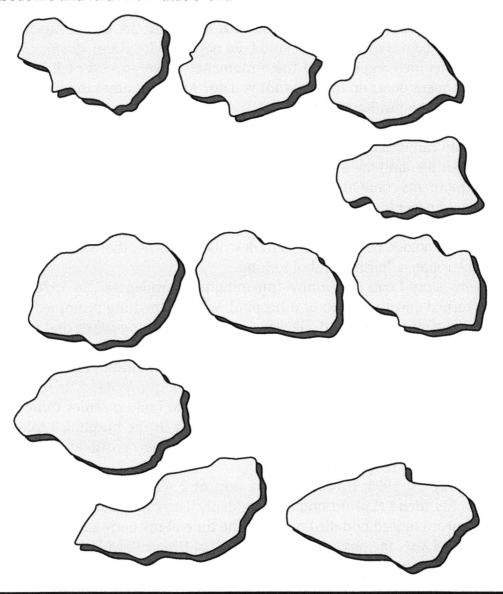

DISCERNING GOD'S PRESENCE IN TRANSITIONS

In the midst of transitions we can discern God's presence. The strange reality is that God is at work in meaningful yet mysterious ways.

The psychologist Carl G. Jung had a lifelong interest in coincidences and coined the word *synchronicity*, which he defined as a "meaningful coincidence." Robert H. Hopcke believes that "such coincidences occur at points of *important transitions* in our life"[6] (italics mine). Coincidences may well be God's way of remaining anonymous. Jacob realized this later after the Bethel experience: "Surely the Lord is in this place—and I did not know it!" (Gen. 28:16).

All of us have experienced these moments. Have you ever felt that life shuts or opens doors no matter what you do? Are there times in your experience when you just happen to be in the right place at the right time? Or you may think of an old friend who hasn't crossed your mind for years, and suddenly you run into the person the next day. You may dream about someone from your life, and the next day that person calls you or writes you a letter. These moments come in an almost unbelievable way, when events happen that could never be predicted, let alone controlled.

Carl Jung had many synchronistic experiences, the most famous being the case of the golden beetle. As a client described a beetle, that very insect flew into the room, a "birth" symbol to Jung.

In my story I can find many "meaningful coincidences." In 1976 I had been turned down for a job at a hospital, when something prompted me to stop by the office of a friend. He was reading the evening paper and noticed an opening for a counselor at a community college. I called, applied, and later got the job, which gave my whole life a new beginning. Chance? Coincidence? No, I prefer to believe it was God at work in my life.

In 1985 we had explored every possible site to build a senior center; we were at a dead end. But that day, while visiting in the hospital, I told the administrator about our problem, and he offered a new possibility: Build the senior center on hospital land.

On May 14, 1998, I awoke with a start at 2 A.M. and remembered my dream: My friend Howard had died suddenly. Later that morning I learned that Howard indeed had died at about the time of my early-morning awakening. At 5 A.M., the pastor called on behalf of Howard's widow to ask me to help with the memorial service.

Look back at your own life story and try to remember such moments. These were the moments when you did not make events happen, but life seemed to flow through you, helped by hidden hands. Be aware in the present when those moments occur.

As you consider the changes and transitions in your life, locate a personal photo album. Photographs reflect ourselves back to us across the years. What memories do the photographs trigger?

Close by reading the "Litany for Storytelling" by Donna Coffman:

Since the beginning of time, stories have been told of the mighty works of God. Even the heavens tell of the glory of God, and the firmament proclaims God's handiwork.

Come and hear and I will tell what God has done for me.

When we tell of the faith of Abraham, Moses, and David; Mary, Jesus, and Paul; Augustine, Luther, and Calvin; grandparents, parents, and friends, we pick up the shuttle lying on the loom of the tapestry of God's interaction with humankind. Each time a story is told, a few rows are woven into this tapestry of time. We become connected, tightly woven into the pattern that began before the world began.

Remember the days of old; consider the years long past. Ask your father and he will inform you; your elders, and they will tell you.

By telling our stories, we see how God has been at work in whatever life has brought to us. Meaning is fashioned from our suffering and pain. Healing comes as we make sense of the collection of seemingly disconnected events. By putting experience into language, we build the stories of faith that inspire endurance in present times.

Your life-filled Word brings order to the chaos of our days. In love you claim us as your own.

As we tell our stories, new directions are often revealed to us. We uncover paths not taken because they were covered with the brambles of daily living. Doors fall open that before seemed locked and sealed by the "shoulds" and "oughts" of life.

I will give thanks to the Lord with my whole heart; I will tell of all your wonderful deeds.

When we share our stories, we leave something of ourselves with others. We prepare the loom for the shuttle of generations to come. A strong foundation is woven that will allow more rows to be added to the pattern long after we have disappeared into the warp and weft of history.

Tell your children of it, and let your children tell their children and their children another generation.

In telling our stories, we discover who we are by knowing where we've been. We are able to fit together the pieces of the puzzles of our lives and make sense of who we are. God's design for our part of the tapestry of time is revealed. We become secure in who we are and accept ourselves. Our common humanity is made known, and we find our place in the family of God.

How blest it is to be a part of God's beloved company.

May you and your descendants know forever God's shalom! Amen.

CHAPTER EIGHT

HEALING OF MEMORIES

We know that all things work together for good
for those who love God,
who are called according to his purpose.
—ROMANS 8:28

In healing of memories, I must make a choice.
Will I let past hurts control me and
keep me acting in self-centered ways,
or will I let the peace and love of the Holy Spirit
control my future?
—DENNIS AND MATTHEW LINN

A woman was telling her four-year-old granddaughter how proud she was the first time her mother let her clean the chimneys of the family's kerosene lamps. Her granddaughter asked, "Grandma, why didn't you turn on the electric light?"

"Well, honey, we didn't have electric lights in those days," her grandmother answered.

"Why didn't you call the telephone company and have them come and fix your lights?"

The woman laughed and said, "Dear, we didn't have any telephones either."

The little girl stared thoughtfully at her grandmother for a moment and then asked, "Grandma, did you know Moses?"

RECALLING YOUR PLACE IN HISTORY

The little girl spoke for many people who have no concept of time outside their own life span. Yet many of us have lived through numerous significant moments of history. Some of those historical moments evoke painful memories. What is your response to each of the following events? Where were you...

- during the Great Depression, 1929–33?
- on December 7, 1941, when Pearl Harbor was attacked?
- on April 12, 1945, when Franklin Delano Roosevelt died?
- on May 5, 1961, when Alan Shepard Jr. became the first American in space?
- on November 22, 1963, when John F. Kennedy was assassinated?
- on April 4, 1968, when Martin Luther King Jr. was assassinated?
- on August 9, 1974, when Richard Nixon resigned as President?
- on July 4, 1976, when the United States celebrated its bicentennial?
- on January 28, 1986, when the space shuttle *Challenger* exploded?
- on November 10, 1989, when the Berlin Wall came tumbling down?
- on February 28, 1991, when the United Nations forces won a victory in the Gulf War?

- on November 25, 1993, when Mandela and DeKlerk signed the new constitution in South Africa, ending apartheid?
- on April 19, 1995, when Timothy McVeigh bombed the Alfred P. Murrah Federal Building in Oklahoma City, Oklahoma?
- on April 20, 1999, when thirteen students and teachers were murdered at Columbine High School in Littleton, Colorado?
- on January 1, 2000, when fears that the new millennium would be accompanied by terrorists went unrealized and the threat of Y2K computer glitches never materialized?
- on September 11, 2001, when terrorists attacked the World Trade Center in New York and the Pentagon in Washington, D.C., killing thousands of civilians?

RECALLING SIGNIFICANT PEOPLE

Looking back at the history we have lived through, the ways we have coped with and survived major changes, can be a significant experience. Even more helpful is to remember people and events that influenced our story. We cannot return to the reality of our past, but we can never leave that reality behind. We are who we are because of the people and events that shaped us. The memories won't fade; they represent realities that made us who we are. As we look back with the eyes of faith on the whole sweep of our lives, sometimes what seemed to be chance meetings become hinge-points in our story. Frederick Buechner has written,

> It is in Jesus...and in the people whose lives have been deeply touched by Jesus,...that we see another way of being human in this world, which is the way of wholeness. When we glimpse that wholeness in others, we recognize it immediately for what it is, and the reason we recognize it, I believe, is that, no matter how much the world shatters us to pieces, we carry inside us a *vision* of wholeness that we sense is our true home and that beckons to us.[1]

One way we experience wholeness in this fragmented world is through the touch of people whose lives reflect the wholeness of Christ. Like the woman in the crowd, we often reach out to touch the hem of others' garments so we can find wholeness. The woman reached out to touch the hem of Christ's garment; her faith and Christ's healing touch brought redemption. Our faith in others and their compassion for us can also bring redemption. Like the woman in the crowd, we hear the words, "Daughter [or son]; your faith has made you well, go in peace."

Many persons in our life journeys have been there for us when we needed to open our hearts and tell someone our story. Thomas Hart says, "Any helping relationship in the context of the Christian faith is a mysterious encounter. God *is* somehow present and at work in it....The helper can properly regard him- or herself as making God present to the other in God's concern, compassion, acceptance, support."[2] This is Paul's meaning when he writes to the Corinthians, "We are therefore Christ's ambassadors, as though God were making his appeal through us" (2 Cor. 5:20, NIV). The calm presence of a person who offers us genuine concern and unconditional acceptance while affirming us as persons enables us to believe that God is love.

The story of Samuel and Eli in Hebrew Scriptures clarifies this reality (1 Sam. 3). When God called to Samuel in the darkness, Samuel did not know with whom he was dealing or how to understand this experience. He needed the help of an older person, a spiritual director, to confirm and clarify that God was speaking to him. Eli told Samuel that when he heard God's call, he should respond, "Speak, LORD, for your servant is listening" (1 Sam. 3:9). God's message to Samuel became clear when Samuel followed Eli's instructions. Often our confusion about God's dealings with us finds clarity only in the company of one who knows God's ways.

Gather photographs of all the loved ones you have lost to death—pictures of parents, grandparents, or other relatives, as well as friends who have touched you. Arrange these pictures on a small altar surrounded by candles. Look into the face of each person who has died and allow time to reflect on his or her influence on your life. Be aware that you are on a journey to meet your loved ones in their own time. In a group setting you may wish to share your feelings about this experience and the way it makes you think about your life today.

We live our lives in the center of a circle filled with light, a light that others have generated through their love and concern. The source of each light beam is a significant person who has touched our life.

Write your name in the center of the circle. Think of significant persons (living or dead) who have touched your life. Write their names around the outer edge of the circle. Now imagine yourself sitting in the center of a circle of light. Imagine these significant persons standing at different points on the circumference of that circle. You look at each of them, and your heart fills with gratitude. You want to thank them for their presence in your life and the way they brought God's grace into your life. In a moment of quiet, thank each person.

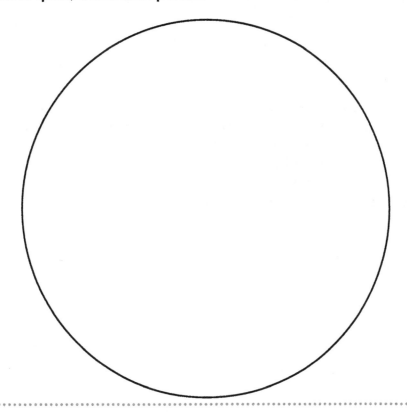

FORGIVING OTHERS

Several biblical scenes remind us of times when forgiveness brought reconciliation. Recall that moment when Jacob and Esau reconciled, their tears bearing witness to their forgiveness of each other. Jacob said, "For to see your face is like seeing the face of God, now that you have received me favorably" (Gen. 33:10, NIV).

Joseph's brothers were helpless in his hands. Years had gone by since he had been victimized by their jealousy and hatred and sold into slavery in Egypt. They were terrified, frightened out of their wits, when he revealed himself as their long-lost brother. But Joseph modeled forgiveness: "But God sent me ahead of you to preserve for you a remnant on earth and to save your lives by a great deliverance" (Gen. 45:7, NIV). Joseph was free of vindictiveness because he saw the pattern of his own life and recognized the providence of God even in his brothers' cruelty.

Recalling early family memories can cause pain. One of the most powerful attachments to our families is the memory of being hurt. Often we become obsessed in later life with memories of injustice, rejection, and sufferings caused by parents. According to Ernest Kurtz and Katherine Ketcham our deepest wounds go back to childhood memories.

> Our pain and sorrow begin at the very beginning, when we begin within our family. Family contains its own paradox, serving on the one hand as shield and protection against newborn vulnerability and, on the other hand, as the setting within which we suffer our first wounds. As infants we are dependent upon our parents to defend and shelter us, yet it is inevitably also our parents who first wound us.[3]

 What "ouches" have you suffered from your parents and siblings?

FORGIVING YOUR PARENTS

As we grow older, we realize our parents did not always love us well. They who loved us also used us and asked much from us in return. However, we must find the grace to overlook our wounds and forgive our parents. The real danger is getting stuck in our resentment. Then we become perennial victims, always complaining that life isn't fair. If you feel your parents caused you undue pain in your childhood, the following exercise may help to repair the relationship.

A LETTER TO PARENTS

Write a letter to your father or mother (or both) dealing with your grievance against them. Express your deepest feelings, but do not send the letter. If either or both parents are deceased, you may wish to carry on an imaginary dialogue with them. It might help to record this dialogue.

We need to acknowledge that our parents are imperfect beings who make mistakes. We may have bitter memories of times when our parents hurt us. Forgiveness does not mean we deny these memories, for they are part of our story. But God's grace transforms them.

FORGIVING OTHERS

A recent example of reconciliation took place in Rome when Pope John XXIII greeted Jewish visitors to the Vatican by descending from his papal throne and embracing them with the words, "I am Joseph your brother." In this simple instance he reenacted the ancient reconciliation between Joseph and his Jewish brothers.

It *is* crucial to forgive those who have caused us pain. We may not be able to forget what happened, but forgiveness releases us from the prison of constantly replaying the event and exacerbating our resentment. Keep in mind Joseph's forgiving spirit as you embark on an exercise that encourages you to forgive persons who have inflicted harm on you. Rabbi Zalman Schachter-Shalomi and Ronald S. Miller talk about planning a "Testimonial Dinner for the Severe Teachers," those who have offended you, to welcome them back into your life, to forgive them, and to acknowledge that the seeming injustice they inflicted on you turned out to be a blessing.[4]

1. Make a list of the people who have hurt you or caused you pain.
   PERSONS WHO HAVE HURT ME OR AGAINST WHOM I BEAR GRUDGES

_____   _____

_____   _____

_____   _____

2. Try to understand the reasons for their actions or your own behavior that may have contributed to your victimization.

3. Freely forgive them, praying for them by name.

4. Thank each of them for what their actions contributed to your growth.

5. If possible, you may wish to phone these persons or write a letter.

In her book *Soul Feast*, Marjorie Thompson suggests that we identify our particular resentments from childhood through the present. She urges us to write them down, identify the cause and effect, and consider how we contributed to the problem.[5] I have chosen a childhood experience because understanding our past helps us see patterns in our adult life more clearly.

Resentment: I resent the fact that my parents made me skip a whole grade when I was nine years old.

Cause: When I entered fifth grade, I felt socially deprived. I felt excluded from social contacts and sports because I was different.

Effect: Loss of confidence, withdrawal, rejection, repressed feelings.

My contribution: I didn't try to make friends or play sports despite my size. I never expressed my unhappiness to my parents.

 In the space below, follow the same process as you deal with a lingering resentment.

Resentment:

Cause:

Effect:

My contribution:

While we may be loath to reopen old wounds, the repair of relationships is important. As Schachter-Shalomi and Miller write,

> What frees us from the tyranny of the past is the understanding that time is *stretchable*, not linear, so we can reframe and reshape it using contemplative techniques....Because it interpenetrates past, present, and future, we can reach back into the past and repair events and relationships that we perceive as failures or disappointments.[6]

Perhaps the wounded child still weeps inside of us, but by doing the work of inner repair we can release ourselves from the prison of a former time.

You may choose to share your painful stories with a spiritual friend. When you do this, something happens. In telling your painful story you receive something in return, namely, your ownership of that experience in a way you have not owned it before. By owning your painful experience, you can then let go of it.

FORGIVING OURSELVES

Healing memories also includes forgiving ourselves. Too often we beat up on ourselves by holding onto our guilt for having hurt other persons. One of my story's most painful memories stems from a time when my oldest son fled college and disappeared.

The incessant conflict between my former wife and me made our home a place of constant warfare. Finally Rick had to get away. On that fateful Thursday he left college, leaving no word of his whereabouts. Friday was the longest day of my life. After checking all possible leads, I returned home immobilized with anxiety. I was sure something terrible had happened to my son.

Two days later my wife and I received a call from Fort Smith, Arkansas. Rick was safe. I made the long trip to drive him back home. What I realized later was that Rick's running away not only asserted his independence but served as a ploy to punish us for our endless bickering.

I had no problem in forgiving Rick for his actions. I understood. But for years I punished myself for my part in his pain. It took reliving the memories, realizing how desperate I was for my own freedom and sanity, and later leaving that marriage before I could let it go and be at peace.

When Peter denied Jesus, Peter went out and wept bitterly (Luke 22:54-62).

The realization of what he had done brought grief and remorse from which he thought he would never recover. How could he ever forgive himself? But then Peter remembered Jesus' words, "Simon, Simon, listen! Satan has demanded to sift all of you like wheat, but I have prayed for you that your own faith may not fail; and you, when once you have turned back, strengthen your brothers" (Luke 22:31-32). Jesus knew Peter would fail, but his prayer was that Peter's faith would not fail. Later Jesus forgave Peter; only then could Peter forgive himself. Beyond his failure was a new beginning.

WHEN RECONCILIATION DOESN'T HAPPEN

Marjorie Thompson has explained the difference between forgiveness and reconciliation. One-way forgiveness releases others from judgment in our own hearts: "[It] release[s] me from the corrosive burden of anger and bitterness that eats away my peace of soul....It removes any hidden or overt effects of resentment in my way of relating to the other....[It] affects the spirit of the person who has been released in ways that go beyond our comprehension or perception."[7]

But reconciliation is a two-way street. Reconciliation means full restoration of a whole relationship and demands a response from both parties (as in the Jacob-Esau story).

Let me set before you two scenes from the Bible where forgiveness did not end in reconciliation. Absalom, David's oldest son, was estranged from his father. His own ambitious lust for power led to a rebellion against the throne. Absalom conspired to seize his father's kingdom and even consented to a plot to kill him (2 Sam. 17:1-4). Though David dearly loved Absalom and forgave him, there was no reconciliation. The last word was the terrible grief of David when he cried, "O my son Absalom, my son, my son Absalom! Would I had died instead of you" (2 Sam. 18:33).

Paul and Barnabas had been close friends and colleagues in the work of the early Christian church. Barnabas had sponsored Paul's reception into the Jerusalem church, brought him to Antioch, and stood by his side on the first missionary journey and at the Jerusalem Council. But Barnabas and Paul had a sharp difference of opinion about taking John Mark on the second missionary journey. "The disagreement became so sharp that they parted company" (Acts 15:39). It was not a friendly parting.

Paul continued to respect Barnabas as a working apostle (1 Cor. 9:6), but the rift was final as far as the record indicates.

At times our forgiveness is one-sided, and reconciliation does not occur because the other person(s) may be unwilling to accept our offer. A man left his marriage of many years, and even when his former wife was vindictive and tried to sabotage his relationship with his children, he did not retaliate. But there was no reconciliation, so he finally had to release this unresolved conflict and move on with his life. A woman had been emotionally abused by her brothers. They rejected her as their sister, never saw her as a person—only an unwelcome intruder into "their" family. Later in life she tried to make peace with her brothers, but they rebuffed every attempt: One brother wanted nothing to do with her, and the other wrote hostile letters. Finally she learned to let go and move on with her own life.

 Can you recall a time in your life when your attempts at reconciliation failed? How did you respond to this failure?

Laurel Mellin tells how there is within most of us a storehouse of leftover anger, sadness and guilt. We recognize these emotions in echoes of childhood's painful memories, scars from disappointments in work or love, losses of innocence, or longings for past roads not taken. Although this "emotional trash" from the past is unavoidable, Mellin believes it is not all bad. She says,

> Retaining some leftover hurts may also encourage the deepening of our own faith. At some point in mid-adulthood, most of us recognize that some life wounds will never completely disappear,

and we consider the possibility that they may be part of a life design that is greater than our own personal intentions. We begin to accept life on its own terms and, by doing so, we may well open up to the will of something greater than ourselves.[8]

So it is that we realize these scars are part of our stories and of a life design beyond our own intentions. In fact, our scars tell our stories! They are road maps that tell the story of our lives. As you read the following meditation, "Scars Tell Our Story," reflect on your own scars, and pray that God will heal your memories.

SCARS TELL OUR STORY

BY RICHARD L. MORGAN

One of the most powerful experiences I have directed recently is "Telling Your Story/Exploring Your Faith" groups with older adults. Everyone has a story to tell, if only there is someone to listen. And those of us in our "third age" of life have a special need to integrate our lives and see how God has been at work in whatever life has brought us.

I have constantly been aware that many of us tell our stories in light of our scars, those experiences that have wounded us and yet transformed us. As one little boy expressed it, "Scars are what you have left after you get well."

Some scars are on our bodies, perpetual mementos of earlier accidents or surgeries. I well remember one of my earliest accidents, which left a major scar. In a church play I played a little dog, and as the chorus sang, "Oh where, oh where has my little dog gone?" I disappeared from sight as I fell off the stage. I still have a scarred chin from that event.

Other scars are on our souls, painful reminders of difficult moments in our lives, where some experience left emotional scars that will always remain. Some bodily scars are on public display, but these emotional scars are hidden in the secret place of our souls. Scars are indeed road maps that tell the story of our lives.

On that memorable eighth day after Easter, Jesus showed Thomas the scars in his hands and side. Like a wounded soldier returning from combat wearing ribbons of victory, the Lord of Life showed the scars of his battle against evil. When Thomas saw the scars, he believed. We praise God that we have a scarred Lord, not a soft and sentimental Jesus, telling sweet stories by the seaside. Those scars remind us that he has been through it all—all that life can do or death destroy.

Only a scarred Christ can relate to our scars. Only a God of scars can understand our wounded world. Jesus' scars remind us of the resurrection faith, that all things that get us down will ultimately be put down. Those "rich wounds, yet visible above" became the place of healing, new beginnings; to our wounds only Christ's wounds can speak.

Our wounds too can be places of new beginnings. There is hope beyond despair for God's Easter people. In our sharing groups many told of the painful scars from their lives, yet it became apparent that at those moments of brokenness God initiated new beginnings. In Hemingway's words in *A Farewell to Arms*, "The world breaks everyone and afterward many are strong at the broken places." Those of us who know what it is to be healed victims also share the joy of becoming wounded healers.

As Christ was known to Thomas by his scars, so we are known by our scars. But there are special scars that ensue from loyalty to Christ. Paul could say of his faith story, "Let no one make trouble for me; for I carry the marks of Jesus branded on my body" (Gal. 6:17).

What do the scars we carry today say about us—not just the ones on display after surgeries and accidents, but those secret scars we hide from view? Scars do tell our story...of broken relationships, shattered dreams, church fights, rejection. But do any of our scars reveal our commitment to Christ? I wonder.

As you remember those who have hurt you and forgive them, pray silently this prayer by John C. Morgan:

> For those whose actions, whether intentional or not, have wounded me. For those whose deeds, whether deliberate or not, have wounded the family of humanity. For those whose words, whether considered or not, have wounded others. For those whose policies, whether reasoned or not, have wounded the world community. For those whose behavior, whether self-conscious or not, has wounded our planet earth. For those whose hearts, whether clear or not, have offended the heart of the cosmos. Grant me: the pain of recognition, the agony of struggle, the comfort of forgiveness, the joy of new beginnings, and the duty of new behavior. Amen.

You may wish to pray the following litany:

A LITANY OF FORGIVENESS

Throughout the biblical story we find many examples of moments when God's people took the initiative in forgiving others.

We remember Joseph, who could have retaliated against his brothers who had wronged him, but who freely forgave them and welcomed them into his family.

We recall how Paul urged the young Christians not to repay evil for evil, heaping burning coals of grace on those who wrong us.

How can we forget the supreme example of our Lord Jesus Christ whose whole life of forgiveness was culminated in those words from the cross, "Father, forgive them; for they know not what they do"?

Even now the painful memories recur…of those who hurt us with cruel words or unjust actions, those who stood silently when others falsely accused us, those who made our lives miserable with their abuse.

Yes, we will think now of these people whose memory still brings pain and hurt.

We reach out to forgive them, as we forgive ourselves for the role we play in this estrangement.

Even as we beg your forgiveness, O God, for thinking more of our hurt than how this brokenness hurts you, Lord, have mercy upon us and restore to us the joy of your salvation. Amen.

AN ONGOING
STORY—
NO EPILOGUE

Thus says the Lord: "Stand at the crossroads,
and look, and ask for the ancient paths,
where the good way lies; and walk in it,
and find rest for your souls."
—JEREMIAH 6:16

Every person is an unfinished story....We dare to
explore the unfinished story we continue to create
until we draw our last breath. Our stories are not
finished....The portrait of our lives remains
unfinished until we breathe for the last time.
—PAULA FARRELL SULLIVAN

*O*ne of the major obstacles to life review is the fear that it signals the end of life. We conjure up an old person writing memoirs as the clock slowly ticks to midnight. But life review is of great value to the dying person of any age. In verbalizing memories, persons can assess the value of their life and come to terms with unresolved conflicts. But one need not equate remembering one's story with the imminence of death.

In *New Passages* Gail Sheehy points out that we live today in the midst of a revolution in the life cycle: "In the space of one short generation the whole shape of the life cycle has been fundamentally altered. People today are leaving childhood sooner, but they are taking longer to grow up and much longer to die."[1] She talks about "the vast New Territories of Second Adulthood," which has two major stages: the Age of Mastery (45–65) and the Age of Integrity (65–85+). The essential questions are these: What will I do with this leftover life? What new ventures or adventures await?

LIFE: AN UNFINISHED STORY

The present never ages. We have been given a gift of these bonus years not only to preserve our life stories but to plan for the future. No longer is retirement that short period of time before frailty and death. It is the Third Age, the Second Middle Age—bright with hope and possibility.

Advances in biomedical science, increased disease prevention, and improved management of chronic diseases have increased our life expectancy. But these leftover years can become a costly victory. Science may extend our life span, but it cannot bring meaning to these years. We need to plan wisely how we will fulfill the time we have saved. Preparation is a priority.

We remember Kierkegaard's quote: "Life can only be understood backwards." But we tend to forget the other clause: "but it must be lived forwards." We do live toward the future, but we must slow down to review past years, to discover the pattern of our lives. Only then can we be clear about how best to live now and in the future.

Looking back is not simply reminiscing; it is looking back to become aware of new possibilities. In that way the future becomes a part of our present being, allowing our present circumstances to shape the future before it happens. The Bible depicts many who were always looking ahead. Jeremiah astounded his contemporaries by buying a piece of real estate in Anathoth at the precise moment when his own country was about to succumb to the Babylonians (Jer. 32:1-15). Jeremiah was investing in the future despite the present difficulties.

Hope is not a vague wish for better things to come but a sense of possibility. Even in times of despair, hope offers a sense of a way out and a destiny that goes somewhere. Our life has purpose. It is not just a series of disconnected events causing other events as haphazardly as a break shot in pool causes billiard balls to career off in all directions. Life has a plan. As Shakespeare says so well in *Hamlet*, "There's a divinity that shapes our ends, rough-hew them how we will."

Viktor Frankl, who found hope for the future, even in the depths of despair in a Nazi concentration camp, wrote,

> All that is good and beautiful in the past is safely preserved in the past. On the other hand, so long as life remains, all guilt and all evil is still "redeemable."...This is not the case of a finished film...or an already existent film which is merely being unrolled. Rather, the film of this world is just being "shot." Which means nothing more nor less than that the past—happily—is fixed, is safe, whereas the future—happily—still remains to be shaped; that is, is at the disposal of [humanity]'s responsibility.[2]

 LOOKING AT YOUR FUTURE

Take time to answer the following questions in the space provided.

Where will you be living ten years from now?

How will you be spending your "free" time?

An old adage says, "The beginning of wisdom comes when a person plants trees, the shade under which they know they will never sit." What present investment of your life will bear future results?

Describe something you have never done that might be a possibility in the next ten years.

Recall a special time in your life story when you were vitally involved in life. What were you doing? Why did you feel so good about your life then?

You may wish to talk about your answers with a friend.

SPIRITUAL REFLECTION

The scriptures throughout call us to remember as a way to plan for the future. One way to facilitate this remembering is to link our stories with the story of the Bible. In *Story Journey* Thomas E. Boomershine claims that the stories of our lives receive power and meaning through their connection with God's story.

We may begin with the Bible story and allow it to be the vessel into which we pour our story, or we can begin with the episodes of our own lives and connect them with Bible stories. Think of some significant experiences in your life from your four ages (Childhood/Youth, Adulthood, Third Age, Fourth Age). In the space provided on page 128, briefly jot down these experiences as you remember them. Then connect your story to a story in the Bible.

For example, a man in his late sixties retired from the business world. He felt that God was calling him to a new venture of faith. After some time and soul searching, his new vocation became clear. He became a financial counselor for nonprofit organizations, donating most of his time. He told me that in a small way his experience paralleled that of Abraham, whom God called in later life to a new venture of faith.

A woman in a nursing home lamented the fact that at first she felt worthless; her active life had ended. However, now she had more time to read the Bible, pray for others, and sit quietly. She recognized that in all those years of continued activity she had been like Martha, serving her family and others. With time for reflection, prayer, and waiting on the presence of God, she now identified with Mary (Luke 10:38-42).

A thirteen-year-old girl troubled her parents because she would sneak a flashlight into bed or get up after others were asleep in order to study her church school and confirmation class materials. She thought it was important to learn the material and become familiar with the things of God. She identified with the story of the young Jesus with the rabbis in the Temple, but she feared ridicule if she admitted this identification. As she matured, she recognized the importance of that story for her faith development. In her mid-forties she entered seminary as a response to this identification. Her ministry of Christian education focuses on children and youth and how they might learn the things of God joyfully.

A weekend retreat on a small mountain in Georgia brought joy and peace and a sense of purpose to fifteen college students. One participant struggled with the wondrous memory of that weekend and the difficulty of coming back down the mountain to the business of college education, part-time work, and troublesome family relationships. *Why couldn't life have stayed so joyful when the experience was over?* he thought. Remembrance of the weekend helped him face other difficult times in his young adulthood, but he wondered why he could not maintain that joyful, uplifting feeling. When he was twenty-seven, he heard a reading of Matthew 17, which tells of the transfiguration of Jesus on a high mountain but then the descent of Jesus and the disciples to face the demands of expectant people. He identified with the disciples who wanted to build booths for Jesus, Moses, and Elijah on the mountaintop, and he realized that even Jesus did not stay on top of the mountain but came back to the experiences of everyday life.

Think of experiences from your various stages of life and then recall a connection to any biblical story. Record the experience and the story in the chart below.

	EXPERIENCE	THE BIBLICAL STORY
Childhood/Youth **First Age** (Birth – 25)		
Adulthood **Second Age** (26 – 50)		
Third Age (51 – 75)		
Fourth Age (76 –)		

Medical science has extended our life span and alleviated some of the chronic illnesses of old age. As we live longer, we face the inevitable health issues that accompany older age. Things just don't work as well as they once did. In *Full of Years* Stephen Sapp underscores this realistic approach to aging when he writes,

The truth is that aging is the deterioration of the organism that *is* the human person, and deterioration, even if inevitable and universal, is hardly something that most people desire or welcome. This decline represents the loss of powers that were previously taken for granted, the loss of much that makes people who they are (or at least have always perceived themselves to be).[3]

In preparation for considering some of the frailties of older age, you may wish to participate in a group experience that will help clarify your values and make you realize some of the issues of older persons. As you reflect on your use of the time before you and the opportunities the future presents, allow this poem by John David Burton to guide your thoughts.

ONCE AGAIN, DIME TIME

On Saturdays, in 1929, I walked up and down

in front of a movie house in Texarkana, Texas,

in my hand a dime hard-earned in cottonfield

or candling eggs on a neighbor's farm.

As I walked I wondered,

"Shall I spend the dime to see Tom Mix and Tarzan of the Apes?"

Sometimes I saved the dime, went off to play

on feed sacks at the general store where

the family was shopping 'til we loaded into

the black Dodge touring car for going home.

When I did go to the picture show, I stayed through twice.

It cost no more and made me think the dime well-spent.

Now, half a century later, I must decide how

to spend not a dime but time—the time left of my life.

What shall I try to get in exchange for what is left of these hurrying years?

The choices are not so simple now,

because I cannot save the time as I could the dime.

Even as I try to decide what to buy with time,

time is running away and I cannot save the time

as I could the dime.

What shall I buy with time?

More of what I have purchased up to now,

regarded by many as a known and reliable quantity in a changing world?

With what time I have left, I can buy some more of that,

and all will say "Amen."

Or is there something else to buy with what time is left,

a moment of joy, adventure equal to that movie house of long ago?

Is there some friend to see, to tell of love,

or a final follow-through with children for which to use what time is left
to me?

On Saturdays long ago, I made the choice to spend or save.

Now, each fleeting day I must choose what to do with hurrying time.

It is "dime time" once again.

 • **How much time do you think you have left?
(Remember your spiritual lifeline.)**

• **Which satisfying leisure-time activities would you like to continue?**

- Which pastimes would you like to forego?

- What material things do you need to give away?

- What new adventures would you like to try?

- What final "follow-throughs" with family or friends do you need to pursue?

. . . .

Mary Jane Stokes wrote a poem that reflects an autumn accounting of her life and indicates that there is always time to "smooth the muss[es] into some semblance of order."

AUTUMN ACCOUNTING

It's not my sins of commission

(there are not many of those)

but my sins of omission

that will damn me—

praises unspoken,
letters unwritten
promises—not broken,
But not fully kept.

I wanted to be like shining silver
like this piece I'm polishing.
The fact remains—I do not shine.
It's not that I'm tarnished,
a trifle dented and bent perhaps,
but not tarnished.
It's simply that I haven't polished
any of my talents to the shine.

I'm more like an unmade bed
lumpy and wrinkled
not very attractive
but suggesting
warmth and comfort,
spent passion
and rest.
Do I have time to smooth the muss
into some semblance of order
spreading the silken coverlet of serenity
over all?
Will anyone wonder what the dust ruffle hides?

How does this poem make you feel?

How will your life end? Will your final days be full of life and your death a sudden interruption? As Eliphaz expressed to Job, "You will come to the grave in full vigor, like sheaves gathered in season" (Job 5:26, NIV). For some this will be the way the end occurs. For others it may involve endless nights and days in an intensive care residential facility with that persistent question on their lips, "Why has the Lord left me here so long?" Either way, death comes to all of us.

Our awareness of our own mortality increases as our circle of friends and family grows smaller. Henri Nouwen and Walter Gaffney write,

> Desolation is the crippling experience of the shrinking of the circle of friends with the devastating awareness that the few years left to live will not allow you to widen the circle again....When they leave you, you know you have to travel on alone. Even to the friendly people you will meet on your way, you will never be able to say, "Do you remember?" because they were not there when you lived it.[4]

Death is no stranger to me, having confronted death many times in my life. As a child of six I was given up for dead when I suffered pneumonia before the advent of "miracle" drugs. I flirted with death when I crawled out of a wreck that totaled my car and only suffered broken ribs and minor cuts. Later in life post-op complications from surgery sent my life to the edge of the precipice.

Weekly I hold the hands of older adults and listen to their dying whispers. I consider it a rare privilege to hear their last words, and I softly relate words of scripture as they leave this world. A person's handling of death is very personal. The "right" answers to the questions How am I supposed to feel? or How am I supposed to act when death comes? do not exist. Everyone will act and react uniquely. However, we must face our own death, not bury its reality and finality.

Zalman Schachter-Shalomi and Ronald Miller claim that many older people live their final days in a box. They suggest that we imagine that every day we take a step toward the Angel of Death: "We are overcome with a primordial terror that makes us recoil from the future....Because we cannot meet death head on, we get anxious and anesthetize ourselves by shutting down awareness. We start reciting an unconscious mantra, 'I don't want to know. I don't want to know. I don't want to know.'"[5] Since we do not want to look ahead, we back into the future. And if we shut down our living connection to the past, we find ourselves "locked in a small box, living a shriveled-up present."[6]

Working through your life story helps you deal with your past. What if we cross the river between life and death to discover that it is another journey, one not totally removed from the experiences of life—but a richer, fuller life? Then our remembering our stories and realizing our faith prepares us for this final journey.

The time has come to deal with your death. Some people have the mistaken belief that contemplating death will hasten its arrival. Nothing is further from the truth. While facing our own death may arouse unwanted, difficult, and even terrifying feelings, death awareness actually energizes us for life. Little wonder then that when asked for the meaning of life, Plato replied, "Practice dying." As we prepare for our aging, so we need to prepare for the final stage of life, our dying.

REFLECTING ON YOUR OWN DEATH

Some people say they are afraid of death; others say they fear dying a slow death. It's not surprising then that we say, "I hope I die of a sudden heart attack rather than a lingering, painful illness." The way we die is unpredictable, but preparing ourselves for death is one of the tasks of life. Death, for Jesus and for us, is that moment in which total defeat and total victory meet. Although the best way to prepare for death is living fully each day, we can prepare for that final moment in several ways.

One of the tasks for a grace-filled death is simplifying life. In my later years I have begun clearing out a lot of my library, giving many books away to libraries and to other clergy. One of my friends wondered if I had suicidal thoughts! Although that is not the case, clearing out my library is a way to practice dying in the midst of life.

Each passing year brings opportunities to clear out the clutter and discard our belongings. De-junking life has spiritual value. Jesus told his disciples as they embarked on their first missionary journey, "Take nothing for your journey" (Luke 9:3). Perhaps we practice part of the act of dying by ridding ourselves of excess baggage that clutters up our lives and prevents us from centering on life's priorities.

You can prepare for death by deciding many practical matters now: living will, durable power of attorney, memorial service plans, and the disposition of your body. Many books and guides will help you make these decisions.[7] The concern now is facing your own death.

 Reflect and respond in writing to the following questions.

- **What historical person's death did you grieve the most? Why?**

- **Whose death in your own experience did you grieve the most? Why?**

- **How did your parents die?**

• **If you could choose, would you prefer to die prior to someone you loved or live after them?**

After answering the questions, read John Burton's poem, "If I Knew I Soon Would Die."

If I knew I soon would die,

I would look at earth and sky

with a wonder not now known

to my busy mind and hurrying eye.

If I were told, "Your time runs out,"

I would try to be about some life

and love which I know I want but day

by day still live without.

If I believed my days were few,

I would ask some time with you

for laughing, loving, talking

the way we sometimes do.

In quiet time I wonder why

I put life off to a by-and-by,

knowing as I do know

that one day I must die.

Take time to describe your feelings about your own death.

Deena Metzger expressed this wish for her death:

> What I ask from my death, is that at the last minute I will be able to look back over my life and know, without any doubt, the entire story I have been living....Then I will know, despite pain, disappointment, and limitation, that this life of mine has been a good and meaningful work.[8]

In a way, you have been preparing for your death by remembering your story and realizing your faith. In Jesus' dying hour his last words on earth were, "It is finished." He could look back on his life and realize that he had accomplished his mission on earth. Write the story of your life in five short, concise sentences. Don't worry about chronology. You may start in the middle or the end. When you have finished, notice what you have included and what you have omitted.

Perhaps through personal experience we have learned the importance of silence when a loved one or friend dies. As we sit with someone, our silent companionship bridges a gap brought by grief. The death of a loved one calls to mind the language beyond words. Elisabeth Kübler-Ross reminds us, "Watching a peaceful death of a human being reminds us of a falling star; one of the million lights in a vast sky that flares up for a brief moment only to disappear into the endless night forever."[9] In that spirit of reverent silence, read the following prayer entitled "Love's Hospice," by George Gunn:

Center your heart on the highest gifts and I will show you the way home.

> *If I speak now with words to eulogize or to trace a godly heritage, but speak of mortality without love, I will sound a death knell and voice no heavenly hope.*

> *And if I have power to predict immortality and to understand the sweet mystery of life and death, and to answer all the ultimate questions;*

> *And if by faith every mounting doubt is conquered and every regret is removed, but I embrace such wisdom and faith without love, I am left with nothing in the final equation.*

> *If I spend my last breath serving others, and look back on my years as an offering to God, but know that life has been poured out without love, I must acknowledge that I have gained nothing that is eternal.*

> *Love in one's last hours waits patiently for that bright appearing and is gentle going into that dark night; it does not covet the lot of the living nor does it storm heaven's gates.*

> *Love at death's door insists only that love's way be affirmed; it is not irritated with its adversaries nor resentful of its helpers; it does not complain but rejoices in all that has been and says yes to all that is to come.*

Love in the twilight bears up, shares the burden of separation; upholds, believes in the words of eternal life; enables, hopes for every promise's fulfillment; embraces, endures all demands to the very end.

Love itself never ends. As for our visions of heaven, they shall fade; as for earthly wisdom, it shall cease; as for certainty of our destiny, it will prove unnecessary.

For what we know is always incomplete and our speculation about the future life is only a guess or a gesture; but when life in its fullness and perfection dawns, the imperfect need no longer satisfy us.

When I began life with a child's eyes on heaven, I spoke as a child, of a heavenly father; I thought as a child, of lambs in a shepherd's arms; I reasoned as a child, of a mother hen with her brood.When I came to more mature years, I gave up such simple ways of speaking and thinking and reasoning.

But now we are looking beyond these dim reflections of reality and are coming to view life and the Life-Giver face-to-face. Once we knew God in a partial way, but now we know God in God's fullness, even as God has always known us.

So faith that brings heaven's joys near to us, hope that dwells on that distant shore, and love that brings God to us; these three abide, always, but the greatest of these is the love that brings us to God.

Take leave with love.

CHAPTER TEN

FINDING THE PATTERN

I have fought the good fight,
I have finished the race, I have kept the faith.
—2 TIMOTHY 4:7

Having done everything,…stand firm.
—EPHESIANS 6:13

Life review yields long-term gains that enrich character
by bringing understanding to events. The patterns in
your life become more discernible among the wreckage
and the romance, more like a well-plotted novel that
reveals characters through their actions and reactions.
—JAMES HILLMAN

*C*laude, now ninety years old, lives in a comfortable room in a nursing home. Although he is frail in body, his spirit is full of life. When he spied me coming to visit, he pointed around his room and said, "See this furniture? It's all mine." It was his way of connecting with his past.

When I asked questions about the faded pictures that lined the walls of his room, Claude's aged eyes brightened. "Wait a minute," he said. "I want to show you my most precious possession." He crept along on his walker, stumbled over a chair, and finally made it to a desk. He dragged out a worn scrapbook and turned page after page of intriguing pictures and clippings from his life story. "It's been a long time ago," he said. "But I had a good life. This scrapbook reminds me of who I was and am."

I left with a prayer of thanksgiving for Claude's life. As I made my way down the nursing home corridors, I could not help but think of my own life. If God spared me to reach that ninetieth year, I too might sit in a confined room amid cluttered memories, showing visitors my memoirs.

On the other hand, Mildred's story was never recorded. She was born in 1899 and lived in three different centuries before her death in the year 2000. At the funeral her family remembered some of the stories of her life, but there were so many gaps. All lamented the fact that they had not recorded her story before it was too late.

We need to preserve our memories, especially since we are blessed with extended years. This is why it *is* so important to remember our stories. Then we, like Claude, can feel a sense of integrity about our lives. Henri Nouwen and Walter Gaffney say life is like a large wheel in which

> No one of its spokes is more important than the others, but together they make the circle full and reveal the hub as the core of its strength. The more we look at it, the more we come to realize that we have only one life cycle to live, and that living is the source of our greatest joy![1]

Like the turning of the wheel, we age; yet there is unity in this one life we live. Now it is time to view the "spokes" of our lives in their wholeness. Often life seems so fragmented that we cannot see the whole picture. Perhaps you are beginning to glimpse the meaning of your life.

REFLECTING

Director Frank Capra's 1946 film, *It's a Wonderful Life*, tells the story of an ordinary man named George Bailey, who despairs that his life has not amounted to anything. Bailey jumps from a bridge, but a guardian angel named Clarence rescues Bailey and shows him the disasters his hometown would have experienced if he had never lived. At the end of his guided tour of George Bailey's past, the angel says, "Strange, isn't it, how a man's life touches so many other lives? When he isn't around, he leaves an awful hole, doesn't he?" George learns to appreciate the positive effect he has had on the people in his life and to realize that his life *has* made a difference!

Complete the following sentence fragment in a short paragraph:

If I hadn't been born....

SEEING THE PATTERN OF OUR LIVES

Abbie, a retired nurse, was one of the first nurses in the United States to work with the iron lung. Her incredible story of a life given to others would have been lost if she had not told it to me, and I had not then recorded it for her on tape. Often as she talked into the tape recorder she was making a quilt. Abbie saw the connection between telling her story and finishing the quilt. "It all makes sense now—what my life really means. It is like making a quilt. The pieces are there, but I need to see the pattern I have made."

In a way our story is like quilting. We start with the scraps of material handed down to us—our genetic makeup, our family history. Then we purchase other materials we can afford to buy with the talents and experiences of life. Some of these pieces are smooth, others jagged. And finally we take all these pieces of material and sew them together, discovering a unique pattern of our own making.

Wayne Oates, in his book *The Struggle to Be Free*, views his life as a struggle to overcome difficulties.[2] He sees his life's wholeness in discovering freedom. In every stage of his life story, he decides to submit to slavery or commit to live creatively in a struggle to be free.

REFLECTING ON YOUR STORY

Think through your life story and see if you can perceive the pattern that ties it together. As you look at the pattern of your life's story, write down your thoughts to the following questions:

1. If you could relive one event in the story of your life, what would it be?

2. Which year would you choose as the best year of your life? Why?

3. Are you the same person you were as a child, or different? Explain.

4. If you could change any part of your life story, what would you change?

5. Can you discern any major turning point in your life that gave new meaning to your story?

WHAT I'D LIKE TO DO OVER AGAIN

Another way to gain insight into your life story is to return in your memory to one special year, a very good year. Revisit its bright moments, pull it from your memory bank, and renew its joy.

What was that year? _____.

Why was it special?

Suppose you had one last message to leave to the handful of people who are most important to you. What would it be in twenty-five words or less?

Of all the things you have done in your life, which is the one you would be most likely to undo?

Which is the one that makes you happiest to remember?

YOUR EPITAPH

Story theologian John Shea has said that "whenever our biographies are deeply probed, a root metaphor appears which gives unity and meaning to our lives."[3] How would you describe the root metaphor "which gives unity and meaning" to your life?

....

When Maggie Kuhn, the energetic founder of the Gray Panthers, died, her epitaph read in this way:

Here lies Maggie Kuhn
Under the only stone she left unturned.

Benjamin Franklin was an omnicompetent man, but his epitaph describes his life's meaning under the rubric of a printer:

The Body of B. Franklin, Printer
Like the cover of an old book,
Its contents torn out
And stript of its lettering and gilding

lies here, food for worms.
But the work shall not be wholly lost
For it will, as he believed, appear once more
In a new and more perfect edition.
Corrected and amended by the Author.

Thomas Jefferson ordered that his epitaph read as follows:

Here was buried Thomas Jefferson
Author of the Declaration of American Independence,
of the Statute of Virginia
for Religious Freedom
and Father of the University of Virginia.

Recently I visited the gravesites of my parents. There was a touch of autumn in the air. Sadness gripped my heart as I glanced at their graves. All that I saw was the dates of their birth and death etched in that barren, cold stone. But then I remembered the haunting words of Kahlil Gibran in *The Prophet*, "Whenever you pass by the field where you have laid your ancestors, look well thereupon and you shall see yourselves and your children dancing hand in hand." Like the worthy woman described in Proverbs, "Strength and dignity [were like] clothing, and [they] laugh at the time to come" (31:25). In some better world my parents too laughed at the time to come, and their children and grandchildren danced...and I was at peace.

 As you try to define the "root metaphor" of your life, how would you write your own epitaph? Try it in the space provided on the next page.

MY MATURE FAITH STATEMENT

Psalm 23 remains the best-known and best-loved passage in the Bible. It is divinely simple and simply divine. I think of it as the faith review of David in his third age. As he reminisced about his past and remembered his story, he came to understand all of his life related to God as the shepherd.

David remembered his childhood and realized that just as he had cared for his sheep, God the shepherd had cared for David's needs, providing green pastures, still waters, and right paths. During David's turbulent years as king of Israel, God remained a loving presence in the valleys of deep darkness. Even the tragic pain David experienced in his own family had not separated him from this relentless friend. Later in life, God was his host and friend, providing sanctuary in the presence of his enemies, shoring him up in the face of the debilities and difficulties of old age.

David used these words to summarize his life story: "Surely goodness and mercy shall follow me / all the days of my life, / and I shall dwell in the house of the Lord my whole life long" (Ps. 23:6). Realizing God's unconditional love liberates us from the image of a ledger-keeping God who condemns people to punishment in this life and the next.

Harry R. Moody and David Carroll, in their book *The Five Stages of the Soul*[4] claim that every person's experience of the stages of the soul differs, although enough similarities exist between individual journeys to identify common patterns. The five stages of the soul are as follows:

1. *The Call.* The Call is known by many names—change of heart, conversion, but basically is a movement from the circumference to the center.

2. *The Search.* The Search begins with a quest for guidance, a spiritual practice that seems right for us.

3. *The Struggle.* After guidance is found, a struggle ensues. Disillusionment, despair, regret, and impatience characterize this "wilderness" experience.

4. *The Breakthrough.* It involves a burst of vision, a new beginning, an experience of joy. Something is changed in us, and we are never the same.

5. *The Return.* Life goes on as before, but there is a difference that makes the ordinary unique. As the Zen proverb tells us, "Before enlightenment you chop wood and carry water. After enlightenment you chop wood and carry water."

In the story of the patriarch Jacob, we can discern these stages of the soul. The Call comes to Jacob at Bethel in the dream of heaven's reaching down to his world. His Search takes him away from home to Haran and twenty years of seeking to integrate this Call into his life. At Peniel the Struggle and Breakthrough occur, as the strange midnight struggle with God brings a breakthrough to a new identity, Israel. Jacob then makes his Return to family and home, a changed man, never again to be the same.

Think about your own faith journey as stages of the soul. Though the stages tend to be sequential, this sequence is not written in stone. You may experience the first stage and go no further.

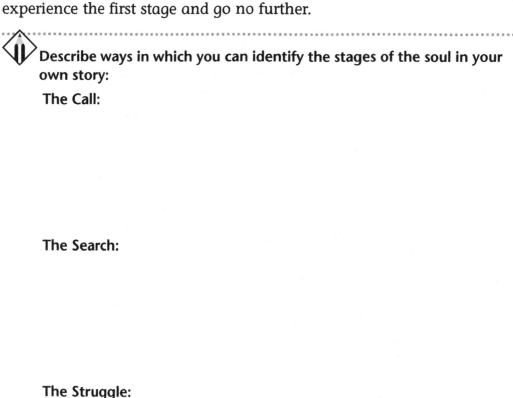

Describe ways in which you can identify the stages of the soul in your own story:

The Call:

The Search:

The Struggle:

The Breakthrough:

The Return:

How do these stages help clarify your own soul story?

· ·

MOVING BEYOND OUR STORIES

The Buddha told his disciples this parable: A man is on a journey. He comes to a vast stretch of water. On this side the shore is dangerous, but the other side is safe and without danger. No boat goes to the other shore which is safe and without danger, nor is there any bridge for crossing over. It would be good therefore if I would gather grass, wood, branches and leaves to make a raft, and with the help of that raft cross over safely to the other side.

Then that man, O disciples, gathers grass, wood, branches and leaves and makes a raft, and with the help of that raft crosses over safely to the other side, exerting himself with his hands and feet. Having crossed over and got to the other side, he thinks: "This raft was of great help to me. With its aid I have crossed over safely to this side. It would be good if I carry this raft on my head or on my back wherever I go."[5]

The Buddha then would ask his disciples what should be done with the raft. Would it not be better to beach the raft on the shore or let it float away? Thus the Buddha would explain that his teachings are for use in crossing over and not for carrying throughout life.

Our stories are priceless treasures from our past. Like the raft, they carry us from nonbeing to awareness in our adult years. Once our story has helped us pay attention to our history—helped us name it and claim it—it is time for us to move on with the rest of our story. Dealing with the past frees us from being stuck and enables us to live our future unbound. We have crossed the river. We need not carry our stories on our backs forever. We begin the incredible journey of writing new stories.

LOOKING BACKWARD AND AHEAD

As you look backward at your experience of remembering your story, you know there is always an untold story for all of us. We all need to find that balance between discretion and disclosure. If you were in a group, your privacy was kept inviolate, as we all have stories that stay within the silent spaces of our lives.

None of us wants to "cast our pearls before swine." It is undesirable, if not impossible, to always wear our hearts on our sleeves, to keep our stories on our lips, and not to take some stories to our graves. William Lowell Randall maintains that when telling our story, there is always the fear of being engulfed by memories, which include "memories of humiliation, of horror, of abduction, of abuse—of that skeleton in our closet, that one unmentionable event that sits like a black hole at the heart of our history, that silent centre round which all our self-storyings must skirt."[6] So we end with some untold stories known only to us and to God.

Although you have reached the close of this study, the end signals a beginning. The journey goes on. The portrait of our lives remains unfinished until we breathe for the last time. Our story has no ending now; there is always the future of the next chapter.

> **You may choose to write in a journal or record your story on videotape. The questionnaire and list of questions in the Appendix will guide you in this task. You will be writing your story as long as you live.**

Recall that memorable Easter afternoon when two of Jesus' disciples walked the seven miles from Jerusalem to Emmaus. A stranger joined them, and they told him the events that had taken place prior to their leaving Jerusalem. The story was one of heartbreak, death, and seemingly final despair. In his turn the stranger illuminated their story with a story of his own. That story and presence transformed them with light and fire: "Were not our hearts burning within us while he was talking to us on the road?" (Luke 24:32).

Al Kreinheder, a Jungian analyst in Los Angeles, who died of cancer in 1990 at the age of seventy-six, writes of our ongoing story:

> There is in each of us an ongoing story. It contains our meaning and our destiny....This is our "soul story."...Though we do not know its final outcome, nor even what will come tomorrow, there is nevertheless a great joy and peace in knowing we are with the story. This is our soul's journey. This is what it means to "live one's soul." This is what life is all about.[7]

Our journey ends, or does it just begin? For now we acknowledge three realities:

1. **We can see all of our past in a new light and with a sense of forgetting that may actually be the truest form of forgiveness and limitless blessing.**

2. **If we have shared stories with others and listened to their stories, we have discovered the blessed community.**

3. **Our stories do not end now but continue as long as we breathe...and beyond.**

James Hillman believes that all our past experiences become more pleasant in life review. "Arduous struggles, envious rivalries, even betrayals come back with a new valence. They don't hurt as much. The musing may even make them amusing. The long illness, the wrong marriage, all the slings and arrows of outrage lose their fire and forget their aim."[8] Hillman also believes that the dark days of the past lighten up as memories are recalled. "Is this a subtle hint that the soul is letting go of the weights it has been carrying, preparing to lift off more easily?"[9]

In a powerful way this truth came home to me recently as I stood on the lonely sands of the beach at Iona, that same beach where Saint Columba landed and often chanted 150 psalms before dawn. The tradition is that you throw a rock into the sea, symbolically casting away old weights from your life. As I hurled a rock into the sea, I felt as if my past had been forgotten and a new future was at hand.

As we have shared our stories, listened to others tell their stories, we have become soul friends. On a deeper level our "soul stories" have brought us into the presence of God's story and into a closer relationship with our greatest friend.

This incredible journey of sharing our stories never ends as long as we live. Our spiritual autobiography remains unfinished. Even as we breathe our last and enter another life, our story continues. For the mirror through which we now see dimly will become clear; we shall know fully, even as we are fully known. And that Holy Presence will go with us into that gentle night.

Celebrate your story!

A LITURGY FOR STORYTELLING
DONOVAN DRAKE

CALL TO WORSHIP

"In the beginning God created the heavens and the earth." Do you remember the story?

Yes! We remember. It was you, Lord, who scratched light out across the surface of darkness. We remember that it was you who swept across the face of the sea. We remember that you, O God, called us into being and made us your people.

You do remember! The story is older. It is older than our bones, kept in faith, kept by faith.

The story surrounds our senses. We remember hearing the laughter of Sarah. We remember seeing old Moses climbing mountains. We remember dry bones rising up. We remember the touch of God's grace.

We thank you for being our God in ages past and for ages to come. Today we celebrate the story that is strong and vibrant in the lives of all people. May the word awaken us all today, so that we may never forget.

CONFESSION

We confess to you, Holy One, that we are blinded by what is new and exciting. We have listened to the world's telling us that our value is found in "youthful appearance." We are instructed to hide the signs of aging. We are summoned to "throw out the old and bring in the new."

We confess that we have allowed age to separate, and we seek forgiveness. Forgive the young when they look at the old with eyes that say, "You have nothing left to offer." Forgive those who are middle-aged when they

believe that the rest of life will be downhill. Forgive those who are old when they have thought too little of their lives simply because of their age.

May those who are old spark the young with vision. May the young seek after those who have found wisdom in the length of their days. Hear our humble confession.

ASSURANCE OF PARDON

We are told that all who humble themselves before God will be exalted. In the humble confession of sin, the Lord promises to renew us. The Lord comes as our strength, granting us wings like eagles, so that we may run and not be weary, that we may walk and not faint.

PRAYERS OF THE PEOPLE

Holy Lord, you are the one who calls this day into patterns. The first strand of morning brightness shines on the sea, bounces off mountain landscapes, fills valleys with light. Light chases darkness across the morning. Darkness chases light into evening. It is the pattern of the day. It has been your creation from age on age.

Lord, you call our days on days into patterns: the child is born, the first day of school, a driver's license, graduation, new jobs, birthdays and promotions, retirement planning, grandchildren and great-grandchildren. You, O Lord, have given us days on days. We pray that we may find each day a gift from you and that we may celebrate your creation.

God of life, as our days on earth accumulate, we pray that we may learn to love the process of aging. Help us know that you have brought us to this time, and it is you who is leading us into the time to come.

Guided, O Lord, by your pattern of love found in Christ, we pray for those who have accumulated wisdom throughout their days. Grant them the courage to share their gifts and grant the young the desire to search for it like hidden treasure.

When age causes separation and loneliness, may a listening ear and gentle touch be found. Grant your "rod and staff" for those who cry in panic from nursing home rooms and from classrooms. Provide "still waters" for persons who are trapped in whirlpools of anxiety. Make memories pleasant for those who have lost the conversation of lifelong friends and good-night kisses.

Grant patience when patience is running low. Grant love when anger holds the heart. Grant encouragement when discouragement drags down.

Lord, may our hearts rest assured on your holy promises, and may the story of love through the ages and for the ages pattern our lives with love, hope, and grace. Amen.

NOTES

FOREWORD

1. Jean Shinoda Bolen, *Crossing to Avalon: A Woman's Midlife Pilgrimage* (San Francisco: HarperSanFrancisco, 1994), 272–73.

PREFACE

1. Michael Vitez, "Write Stuff," *Philadelphia Inquirer*, 20 February 2000.

CHAPTER 1—FROM MEMORY TO FAITH: LIFE STORIES

1. Henri J. M. Nouwen, *The Life of the Beloved: Spiritual Living in a Secular World* (New York: Crossroad Publishing, 1992), 54.

2. Frederick Buechner, *Telling Secrets* (San Francisco: HarperSanFrancisco, 1991), 30.

3. Thomas E. Boomershine, *Story Journey: An Invitation to the Gospel As Storytelling* (Nashville, Tenn.: Abingdon Press, 1988), 198.

4. Thomas N. Hart, *The Art of Christian Listening* (Ramsey, N.J.: Paulist Press, 1980), 1.

5. Henri J. M. Nouwen, "Care and the Elderly," in Carol and Perry LeFevre, eds., *Aging and the Human Spirit* (Chicago, Ill.: Exploration Press, 1981), 326.

6. C. G. Jung, *Memories, Dreams, Reflections*, rev. ed., edited by Aniela Jaffé and translated by Richard and Clara Winston (New York: Pantheon Books, 1973).

7. Wendy Lustbader, *What's Worth Knowing* (New York: Jeremy P. Tarcher/Putnam, 2001), 200.

8. Sam Keen, *Hymns to an Unknown God* (New York: Bantam Books, 1994), 43.

CHAPTER 2—THE SPIRITUAL LIFELINE

1. *Maggie Kuhn on Aging: A Dialogue*, edited by Dieter Hessel (Philadelphia: Westminster Press, 1977), 31.

2. Dan Wakefield, *The Story of Your Life* (Boston: Beacon Press, 1990), 93.

3. John S. Dunne, *A Search for God in Time and Memory* (Notre Dame, Ind.: University of Notre Dame Press, 1977), viii.

CHAPTER 3—THE RIVER OF LIFE

1. Morton T. Kelsey, *Adventure Inward: Christian Growth through Personal Journal Writing* (Minneapolis: Augsburg Publishing House, 1980), 141–42.

2. Norman F. Maclean, *A River Runs through It* (Chicago: University of Chicago Press, 1976), 104.

3. William Stafford, "Ask Me," in *The Way It Is: New & Selected Poems* (Saint Paul, Minn.: Graywolf Press, 1988), 56.

CHAPTER 4—RECLAIMING CHILDHOOD STORIES

1. William M. Clements, "Spiritual Development in the Fourth Quarter of Life," *Journal of Religious Gerontology* 7 (1990): 66.
2. Frederick Buechner, *A Room Called Remember* (New York: Harper & Row, 1984), 4.
3. Buechner, *Telling Secrets*, 10.
4. Ibid., 22.
5. Merle R. Jordan, *Reclaiming Your Story: Family History and Spiritual Growth* (Louisville, Ky.: Westminster/John Knox Press, 1999), 1.
6. Roberta C. Bondi, *Memories of God: Theological Reflections on a Life* (Nashville, Tenn.: Abingdon Press, 1995), 67.
7. Ibid., 35.

CHAPTER 5—FAMILY RELATIONSHIPS, FAMILY STORIES

1. Buechner, *Telling Secrets*, 43.
2. Monica McGoldrick, *You Can Go Home Again: Reconnecting with Your Family* (New York: W. W. Norton & Co., 1995), 22.
3. Michael E. Williams, "Voices from Unseen Rooms: Storytelling and Community," *Weavings: A Journal of the Christian Spiritual Life* 5 (July/August 1990): 19.
4. Henri J. M. Nouwen, *The Return of the Prodigal Son* (New York: Doubleday, 1992), 105.
5. Gregory Bateson, cited in McGoldrick, *You Can Go Home Again*, 287–8.

CHAPTER 6—STORIES CONNECT GENERATIONS

1. John O'Donohue, *Eternal Echoes: Exploring Our Yearning to Belong* (New York: Harper Collins, 1999), 37, 38.
2. Jack Maguire, *The Power of Personal Storytelling: Spinning Tales to Connect with Others* (New York: Jeremy P. Tarcher Publishers, 1998), 196.
3. Mary Pipher, *Another Country: Navigating the Emotional Terrain of Our Elders* (New York: Riverhead Books, 1999), 306.
4. McGoldrick, *You Can Go Home Again*, 36.
5. William Strauss and Neil Howe, *Generations: The History of America's Future, 1584 to 2069* (New York: William Morrow & Company, 1991), 28–32.
6. Jack Riemer and Nathaniel Stampfer, *So That Your Values Live On: Ethical Wills and How to Prepare Them* (Woodstock, Vt.: Jewish Lights Publishing, 1991), 232.
7. Kathleen Fischer, *Winter Grace: Spirituality and Aging* (Nashville, Tenn.: Upper Room Books, 1998), 73–4.

CHAPTER 7—FACING LIFE'S TRANSITIONS

1. Paul W. Pruyser, "Aging: Downward, Upward, or Forward?" *Pastoral Psychology* 24 (winter 1975): 102–18.
2. Carl G. Jung, *Psychological Reflections: A New Anthology of His Writings, 1905–1961*, edited by Jolande Jacobi (Princeton, N.J.: Princeton University Press, 1970), 137–38.
3. William Bridges, *Transitions: Making Sense of Life's Changes* (Reading, Mass.: Addison-Wesley Publishing, 1980).
4. William Bridges, "Getting Them through the Wilderness: A Leader's Guide to Transition" (unpublished training material).
5. Bridges, *Transitions*, 112.
6. Robert H. Hopcke, *There Are No Accidents: Synchronicity and the Stories of Our Lives* (New York: Penguin Putnam, 1997), 23.

CHAPTER 8—HEALING OF MEMORIES

1. Frederick Buechner, "Journey toward Wholeness," *Theology Today* 49 (January 1993): 457.
2. Hart, *The Art of Christian Listening*, 9.
3. Ernest Kurtz and Katherine Ketcham, *The Spirituality of Imperfection* (New York: Bantam Books, 1994), 228.
4. Zalman Schachter-Shalomi and Ronald S. Miller, *From Age-ing to Sage-ing: A Profound New Vision of Growing Older* (New York: Warner Books, 1995), 279–80.
5. Marjorie J. Thompson, *Soul Feast: An Invitation to the Christian Spiritual Life* (Louisville, Ky.: Westminster John Knox Press, 1995), 88.
6. Schachter-Shalomi and Miller, *From Age-ing to Sage-ing*, 93.
7. Marjorie J. Thompson, "Moving toward Forgiveness," *Weavings: A Journal of the Christian Spiritual Life* 7 (March/April 1992): 21.
8. Laurel Mellin, "Taking Out Your Emotional Trash," *Spirituality and Health* (spring 2000): 34.

CHAPTER 9—AN ONGOING STORY—NO EPILOGUE

1. Gail Sheehy, *New Passages* (New York: Random House, 1995), 4.
2. Viktor Frankl, *The Doctor and the Soul* (New York: Vintage Press, 1986), 34–35.
3. Stephen Sapp, *Full of Years* (Nashville, Tenn.: Abingdon Press, 1987), 135.
4. Henri J. M. Nouwen and Walter Gaffney, *Aging: The Fulfillment of Life* (New York: Image Books, 1974), 36–7.
5. Schachter-Shalomi and Miller, *From Age-ing to Sage-ing*, 89.

6. Ibid., 90.

7. See Barbara Karnes, *Gone from My Sight: The Dying Experience,* for guidelines about the dying experience. Available from Barbara Karnes, RN, P. O. Box 335, Stillwell, Kansas 66085.

8. Deena Metzger, *Writing for Your Life* (New York: HarperCollins, 1993), 49.

9. Elisabeth Kübler-Ross, *On Death and Dying* (New York: The Macmillan Company, 1970), 276.

CHAPTER 10—FINDING THE PATTERN

1. Nouwen and Gaffney, *Aging: The Fulfillment of Life,* 13.

2. Wayne Oates, *The Struggle to Be Free: My Story and Your Story* (Philadelphia, Pa.: Westminster Press, 1983).

3. John Shea, *Stories of God: An Unauthorized Biography* (Chicago: Thomas More Press, 1978), 56.

4. Harry R. Moody and David Carroll, *The Five Stages of the Soul: Charting the Spiritual Passages That Shape Our Lives* (New York: Doubleday, 1997).

5. Cited in Wayne Muller, *How, Then, Shall We Live?* (New York: Bantam, 1996), 36–37.

6. William Lowell Randall, *The Stories We Are: An Essay on Self-Creation* (Toronto: University of Toronto Press, 1995), 288.

7. Al Kreinheder, *Body and Soul: The Other Side of Illness* (Toronto: Inner City Books, 1991), 57–58.

8. James Hillman, *The Force of Character: And a Lasting Life* (New York: Random House, 1999), 93.

9. Ibid.

FOUR AGES QUESTIONNAIRE

THE FIRST AGE (BIRTH–25)
CHILDHOOD

1. What is your earliest memory from childhood?
2. Where and when were you born? Can you recall any stories your parents or relatives told you about your birth?
3. How did you get your name?
4. What childhood nicknames can you recall? How did they make you feel?
5. What family stories, jokes, or anecdotes do you remember from those early years?
6. Take an imaginary walk through your childhood town. What memories return?
7. Did you have a secret place as a child? How would you describe it?
8. Recall your first day at school. What was it like?
9. What was your happiest memory as a child?
10. Can you recall any memories of your grandparents? If so, tell them.
11. Recall a favorite Bible story from childhood.
12. Did you go to church as a child? What was that experience like for you?
13. What mental picture of God did you have as a child?
14. What were the rules in your family, the "shoulds" and "oughts"?
15. What would you say were some of the religious traditions of your parents?
16. What were your parents like when you were a child?
17. Did you have brothers and sisters? If so, tell some stories about them.
18. To which family member(s) were you closest? In whom did you confide?
19. In your family who was the clown? the scapegoat? the nurturer? the hero? the lost child?
20. Whom in your family were you most like? in what way?

THE TEEN YEARS

21. Write the word *Teenager* on a blank piece of paper, and then jot down every feeling that comes to mind about those years of your life.
22. What was your most embarrassing moment as a teenager?
23. What was your happiest time during your teenage years?
24. Who were the most important people for you? Whom did you admire, feel close to, want to be like?
25. How did you feel about your parents during those years?
26. Can you describe your first "crush" or attraction during these years? Describe him or her.
27. Describe your first job.
28. What were significant memories of junior high school (middle school) or high school?
29. As a teenager what did you fantasize about being when you were older?
30. What significant memories stand out from your college years (if applicable)?
31. Did you attend church as a teenager? What was that experience like?
32. If you were confirmed during these years, what did that mean for you?
33. Reflect upon your baptism. How old were you? If you were baptized as an infant, have your family members told the story of your baptism? If you do remember your baptism, what do you remember of that experience?
34. Were there times during these years when you wanted nothing to do with God or anything religious? Explain.
35. Can you recall any minister or teacher who influenced you?
36. If you attended college, did you take a college course in religion or the Bible? Did you find any conflict between these courses and what you learned in church school?
37. When was the first time that you remember experiencing the presence of God? Briefly describe what it was like and your age at the time of the experience.

THE SECOND AGE (26–50)

38. Jot down the major events of your early adulthood (ages 26–35). Don't worry about chronological order; just jot them down.

39. Jot down the major events of your later early adult years (36–50) and make note of what seemed to dominate these years.

40. Did you marry? If so, describe the kind of marriage you had. Were you married more than once? Discuss.

41. Write the word *Crisis* in the center of a blank piece of paper. Write as many words as come to mind, circling each one and connecting each word to the previous word. Take another piece of blank paper and write the first thing that comes to your mind.

42. List the various jobs you had during these years, and describe the transitions.

43. What major turning points or transitions did you experience during these years?

44. Tell about your children (if applicable). Recall memories of their birth and childhood.

45. Find an old photo album from these years, and describe the feelings that the photographs evoke.

46. What books or television programs influenced you during these years?

47. How did it feel when you realized your parents were growing older?

48. What was church life like during these years?

49. Tell about a significant event in your life that influenced your faith.

50. What religious books influenced you?

51. Did your understanding of God change from earlier years? If so, how?

52. As you reflect on your faith journey, when has God seemed distant, removed, or absent? When did your spiritual life seem arid or dry?

53. Recall moments of sickness or loss during these years. How did your faith relate to these crises?

54. Recall some specific moments when you prayed. What was the occasion, and how were those prayers answered?

55. What values or beliefs do you no longer hold that you once did?

56. To whom did you turn in moments of great struggles? Why?

57. Did you ever have what some might call a "religious experience"? If so, describe that experience and what it has meant for you.

58. What would you say was the central value or philosophy by which you lived in these years?

59. Did you experience a midlife crisis? If so, how?

THE THIRD AGE (51–75)

60. If you had children, what was it like when they left home?
61. Did you plan for retirement? How did you want to fill your free time once retired?
62. What was (is) your marriage like?
63. What was it like to become a grandparent (if applicable)?
64. What are the best things about your current age? the worst things?
65. Have you had a major illness or surgery during these years? If so, describe that experience(s).
66. What do you hope for as you grow older?
67. What are your fears now?
68. At what times in these years has prayer been the easiest for you? At what times did you find it most difficult?
69. What broken relationships need healing? Describe them.
70. What new skills or interests might you have in this third age?
71. Who are the people you want to spend the most time with now?
72. What skills and talents can you give back to society now? Where do you find "vital involvement"?
73. What present values and beliefs do you hold that will never change?
74. What values or beliefs do you no longer hold that you once did?
75. What is your image of God now? How has it changed from earlier years?
76. Name some persons who have been "spiritual friends" across the years. How did they bring God's grace to you? Why were they role models for you?
77. Recall some Bible stories or texts that have meant a lot to you in your spiritual journey.
78. Recall a major crisis from these years that tested your faith. Can you discern God's presence in those moments?
79. If you could place five books that have influenced your life in a church library, what would they be?
80. Describe your faith in three sentences.

THE FOURTH AGE (76–)

81. What are some of the losses you have experienced in this age, and how did you cope with them?
82. What health issues have you faced? How have you coped with them?
83. List the three major satisfactions of your life.
84. List the three major surprises of your life.
85. List the three major disappointments of your life.
86. What would it be like for you to go to a nursing home?
87. How do you envision your own death? When will it happen?
88. How often do you think about your own death? Explain.
89. If you are married, would you choose to outlive your spouse? Explain.
90. Whom do you want with you when you die?
91. If you had a choice, what kind of death would you prefer?

    tragic

    sudden

    quiet, dignified

    slow and painful

    in the line of duty

    other
92. Looking back on your life story, can you recall someone's death that had a profound effect on you?
93. At what age did your parents die? How did they die?
94. What gifts can you claim that were theirs that will live on through you? What story best depicts who they were?
95. What do you hope your last years on earth will be like? Where will you be?
96. As you reflect on your life, has there been any one way in which God has consistently related to you?
97. Write a letter to a young person stating your philosophy of life.
98. Right now what Bible story or text means the most to you?
99. What does prayer mean to you now? Explain.
100. If you were writing your autobiography for publication, what would be the title of that book?

Videotaping Life Stories

Before the interview ask the person to read through the twenty questions and to gather some pictures of his or her parents and family members as well as other memorabilia. Create a quiet, comfortable, well-lighted, and relaxed atmosphere for the interview. It is important to follow the suggested lead-ins and slowly build memory upon memory, drawing out the interviewee's experiences and life events that illustrate the theme of your guided interview.

Begin each interview with the following: "This is the family history of_____(name). The interviewer is _____ (name); the videographer is _____(name)." Ask the interviewee to state his or her name, address, and date of birth.

Keep in mind that the interview is a guided conversation or discussion. Good, open-ended questions and statements are important for successful interviews. The following lead-ins will serve that purpose.

TWENTY QUESTIONS FOR OLDER ADULTS

1. What is your earliest memory from childhood?
2. Can you recall any family stories, jokes or anecdotes from those earlier years?
3. What were your parents like when you were a child?
4. Whom in your family were you most like, and why?
5. What was your happiest time during your teenage years?
6. Whom did you admire, feel close to, or want to be like in your teen years?
7. What are some significant memories of junior high or high school?
8. Can you recall any significant religious experience during these years?
9. List the most important events of your early adulthood (26–50 years).
10. Did you marry? If so, describe your marriage. Were you married more than once? Discuss.
11. What major turning points do you remember from those years of early adulthood?

12. Did your understanding of God change from earlier years? If so, how?
13. Tell about your children (if applicable).
14. During your Third Age (51–75) what have been some of the best moments? the worst moments?
15. Name some people who have been spiritual friends for you across the years.

    How did they bring God's grace to you?
16. What broken relationships need healing?
17. List the three major satisfactions of your life and the three major disappointments.
18. What health issues have you faced? How did you cope with them?
19. How would you tell a young person about your values?
20. Tell the story of your life in five sentences.

Resources

Albert, Susan W. *Writing from Life: Telling Your Soul's Story*. New York: The Putnam Publishing Group, 1997.

Birren, James E., and Donna E. Deutchman. *Guiding Autobiography Groups for Older Adults*. Baltimore, Md.: Johns Hopkins University Press, 1991.

Birren, James E., and Kathryn N. Cochran. *Telling the Story of Life through Guided Autobiography Groups*. Baltimore, Md.: Johns Hopkins University Press, 2001.

Broyles, Anne. *Journaling: A Spiritual Journey*. Nashville, Tenn.: The Upper Room, 1999.

Buechner, Frederick. *Listening to Your Life: Meditations with Frederick Buechner*. San Francisco: HarperSanFrancisco, 1992.

Erickson, Carolly. *Arc of the Arrow: Mapping Your Spiritual Journey*. New York: Pocket Books, 1998.

McAdams, Dan P. *The Stories We Live By*. New York: The Guilford Press, 1997.

Mandelker, Amy, and Elizabeth Powers, eds. *Pilgrim Souls: A Collection of Spiritual Autobiographies*. New York: Simon and Schuster, 1999.

Morgan, Richard L., "Small Group Spiritual Autobiography Writing and Aging," in Susan McFadden and Melvin Kimble, eds., *Aging, Spirituality and Religion*. Minneapolis, Mn.: Augsburg Press, 2002.

Rainer, Tristine. *Your Life As Story*. New York: Jeremy P. Tarcher and Putnam, 1998.

Randall, William L., *The Stories We Are: An Essay on Self-Creation*. Toronto: University of Toronto Press, 1995.

Ray, Ruth E. *Beyond Nostalgia: Aging and Life Story Writing*. Charlottesville, Va.: The University Press of Virginia, 2000.

Rosenbluth, Vera. *Keeping Family Stories Alive: Discovering and Recording the Stories and Reflections of a Lifetime*. Rev. ed. Point Roberts, Wash.: Hartley & Marks, 1997.

Schachter-Shalomi, Zalman, and Ronald S. Miller. *From Age-ing to Sage-ing: A Profound New Vision of Growing Older*. New York: Warner Books, Inc., 1995.

Stone, Richard. *The Healing Art of Storytelling: A Sacred Journey of Personal Discovery*. New York: Hyperion Press, 1996.

Wakefield, Dan. *The Story of Your Life: Writing a Spiritual Autobiography*. Boston: Beacon Press, 1990.

Scriptural Index for *Remembering Your Story*

Index

ABOUT THE AUTHOR

RICHARD L. MORGAN, an ordained Presbyterian minister, is a national leader in spiritual autobiography groups and spirituality of aging issues. He is the author of several books in the field of aging and has been leading groups across the nation for the past twenty years. He also serves as a consultant to churches that wish to form spiritual autobiography groups.

The publisher gratefully acknowledges permission to reprint the following copyrighted material:

"Once Again, Dime Time" and "If I Knew I Soon Would Die" from *Naked in the Street: Selected Poems of John David Burton*. Used by permission of the author.

"Litany for Storytelling." Used by permission of Donna B. Coffman.

"As We Look Back in Memory." Used by permission of Edith Sinclair Downing.

"A Liturgy for Storytelling." Used by permission of Donovan Drake.

Excerpts from "The Fall of 1972." Used by permission of Steven P. Eason.

"Sometimes." Used by permission of Geraldine A. Goss.

"Love's Hospice." Used by permission of George Gunn.

Excerpts from *The Force of Character* by James Hillman. Copyright © 1999 Random House. Used by permission of James Hillman.

"Prayer of Thanksgiving for the Seasons of Life." Used by permission of Sarah Hipps.

Excerpt from *What's Worth Knowing*. Copyright © 2001 by Wendy Lustbader. Used by permission of the author.

"Prayer" by John C. Morgan from *Prayerfulness*. Used by permission of the author.

"Scars Tell Our Story" by Richard C. Morgan. Used by permission of *Mid-Atlantic Presbyterian*.

"A Litany for the Generations." Used by permission of Dwyn M. Mounger.

Excerpt from "Turning/To the Women, for D.L.D" by Jan L. Richardson in *Sacred Journeys*. Copyright © 1995 by Jan L. Richardson. Used by permission of Upper Room Books.

Excerpt from *So That Your Values Live On: Ethical Wills and How to Prepare Them*. Copyright © Jack Riemer and Nathaniel Stampfer (Woodstock, VT: Jewish Lights Publishing, 1991) $17.95pb+$3.50s/h. Order by mail or call (800-962-4544 or online at www.jewishlights.com. Permission granted by Jewish Lights Publishing, PO BOX 237, Woodstock, VT 05091.

"Ask Me." Copyright ©1977, 1998 by the Estate of William Stafford. Reprinted from *The Way It Is: New & Selected Poems*. Used by permission of Graywolf Press, Saint Paul, Minnesota.

"Autumn Accounting" from *Aging & Spirituality* (Winter 1993). Used by permission of Mary Jane Stokes.

"The Last Spring of My Grandmother." Used by permission of Nancy Yost.